THE ABOLITIONISTS

AMERICAN PROBLEM STUDIES

Under the editorial direction of
OSCAR HANDLIN

THE ABOLITIONISTS

Reformers or Fanatics?

Edited by **RICHARD O. CURRY**
University of Connecticut

HOLT, RINEHART AND WINSTON
New York • Chicago • San Francisco • Toronto • London

Cover illustration: "Last Moments of John Brown," from an etching made in 1885 by Thomas Hovenden *(The Granger Collection).* Illustration on page vi: A page from the *Emancipator,* September 2, 1839 *(The Bettmann Archive).*

CONTENTS

EMANCIPATOR—*EXTRA.*

NEW-YORK, SEPTEMBER 2, 1839.

American Anti-Slavery Almanac for 1840.

The seven cuts following, are selected from thirteen, which may be found in the Anti-Slavery Almanac for 1840. They represent well-authenticated facts, and illustrate in various ways, the cruelties daily inflicted upon three millions of native born Americans, by their fellow-countrymen! A brief explanation follows each cut.

The peculiar " Domestic Institutions of our Southern brethren."

Selling a Mother from her Child.

Mothers with young Children at work in the field.

A Woman chained to a Girl, and a Man in irons at work in the field.

" They can't take care of themselves"; explained in an interesting article.

Hunting Slaves with dogs and guns. A Slave drowned by the dogs.

Servility of the Northern States in arresting and returning fugitive Slaves.

INTRODUCTION

The abolitionist crusade against slavery which began in the 1830s was characterized by religious fervor, a sense of moral urgency, and a vision of human perfection. At first abolitionism was only one of many proposed reforms aimed at providing American society with a new moral and ethical basis. In the early part of the decade, in addition to condemning slavery, reformers actively supported a variety of other causes including temperance, the improvement of public education, and the establishment of asylums for the insane and homes for females who had "Deviated from the Paths of Virtue." But abolitionism ultimately came to overshadow them all.

Opposition to slavery was not a new phenomenon in American history. During the colonial period, Quakers and some members of pietistic sects had condemned slavery on the ground that it was incompatible with the principles of Christianity. And the American Revolution, with its emphasis on the "natural rights" of *all* men to "life, liberty, and the pursuit of happiness," led to abolition or the passage of gradual emancipation laws in every Northern state by 1804. Moreover, Congress excluded slavery from the Northwest Territory in 1787, outlawed the international slave trade in 1808, and, as a result of the Missouri Compromise in 1820, barred slavery north of 36' 30° in the Louisiana Purchase territory. Thus, the abolitionist movement of the 1830s may be considered a logical culmination of an earlier antislavery tradition. But it was more than that.

Most antislavery groups in the late eighteenth and early nineteenth centuries had been disposed toward gradualism and the use of indirect methods in attacking slavery. They advocated, for example, the colonization of freed slaves in Africa and opposed the geographical expansion of slavery. The abolitionists, however, were militant antislavery radicals who condemned slavery as a sin and called for immediate action to eradicate this evil from American life.

Launching a crusade against slavery proved a formidable task. Encountering hostility at every turn, the abolitionists found themselves condemned as fanatics, members of a "lunatic fringe" in American society. William Lloyd

1

Garrison wrote that he found "contempt more bitter, opposition more stubborn, and apathy more frozen" in New England than in the South itself. Nevertheless, the movement thrived. By 1836 there were at least 500 abolition societies in the free states, and by 1840 these societies had a membership of at least 150,000 persons. The abolitionists did not always agree among themselves as to what their aims, objectives, and strategy should be. Garrison often spent as much time attacking the methods and ideology of abolitionists who disagreed with him as he did in attacking the institution of slavery itself. But in spite of divisions in their ranks and vilification and abuse by a hostile public, the abolitionists were a dedicated minority that could not be silenced.

Abolitionism, a disruptive force in the pre-Civil War United States, posed difficult questions for contemporaries, and it is no less controversial today. In the selections that follow, modern historians debate fundamental questions about the origins, significance, and effects of abolitionism on American society.

The traditional interpretation of the movement, formulated primarily in the writings of Garrisonian abolitionists like Wendell Phillips, Oliver Johnson, and Parker Pillsbury, is a simple one. These men viewed abolitionism as an organized religious crusade centered in New England under Garrison's leadership. Garrison, like the prophets of old, was raised up by the Almighty to lead a holy crusade to rid the nation of the sin of slavery. But slaveholders, refusing to be moved by moral suasion and the principles of "true religion," made compromise impossible. Slavery, at war with the laws of God and nature, thus perished by the sword.

Most late nineteenth- and early twentieth-century historians—including James Ford Rhodes, John Bach McMaster, Hermann von Holst, and James Schouler—accepted the Garrisonian or traditional New England interpretation with few reservations. Although none emphasized the intervention of "Divine Providence" into the slavery crisis, all agreed that human bondage was intolerable in a democratic society and praised Garrison and his disciples for their uncompromising stand against the tyranny of the slavocracy. Rhodes is perhaps the most distinguished of these historians. A key passage from his multivolume *History of the United States* (1892–1922) opens debate in this book.

Gilbert H. Barnes was not the first historian to question the validity of explaining the origin and significance of abolitionism in Garrisonian terms, but his revisionist study, *The Antislavery Impulse, 1830–1844* (1933), is a landmark in abolition historiography that influenced a generation of scholars. According to Barnes, abolitionism was indeed a religious crusade, but it was not centered in New England under Garrison's leadership. Rather, it originated with the evangelical revivals of Charles Grandison Finney in the west—western Pennsylvania, Ohio, and the "burned over" district of western New York. Garrison, far from being the chief abolitionist, was not even a typical one. Among the real leaders of the movement, Barnes maintains, were James G. Birney, the

Liberty Party candidate for president in 1840 and 1844; Arthur and Lewis Tappan, wealthy New York philanthropists; and above all, Theodore Dwight Weld, the "movement's man of power, the greatest individual factor in its triumph."

How does Barnes account for Garrison's "unwarranted reputation" as the chief architect and organizer of abolitionism? And why does he conclude that Garrison was more of a liability than an asset to the national movement? "Over the entire agitation," Barnes asserts, Garrison's "name cast a vague and indefinite odium which hampered its growth from the beginning."

Barnes's work is paralleled in many ways by that of Dwight L. Dumond. Dumond, like Barnes, emphasizes the impact of evangelical revivalism in explaining the origin of western abolitionism, and he is extremely critical of Garrison. However, in explaining the rise of militant abolitionism, he stresses the importance also of impulses other than evangelicalism: westward migration, the advent of political democracy, and the aggressive designs of the "slave power." Dumond's work, though distinctive, supplements that of Barnes by adding new dimensions to the western revival thesis.

The selection by Dumond focuses attention on contributions made by Southern "exiles" in providing leadership for the abolitionist movement during the 1830s. How does he explain the decision of thousands of Southerners to seek refuge in the free states? And what does this exodus reveal, according to Dumond, about the nature and character of the crusade against slavery?

While the revisionist ideas of Barnes and Dumond have had an unmistakable influence on abolitionist historiography, the relative importance of western abolitionism as compared with Garrison's New England movement remains a controversial question. Some recent historians, notably Elaine Brooks and Roman J. Zorn, have vigorously reasserted the idea of Garrisonian pre-eminence in the movement.[1] Russell B. Nye, on the other hand, has tried to resolve interpretive differences among historians of abolitionism by attempting a synthesis combining elements from both western revival and New England schools of thought.[2] John L. Thomas, a recent biographer of Garrison, finds still another way to resolve interpretive difficulties created by this lack of consensus. At first glance he appears to provide a synthesis in that he stresses the importance of both western and New England groups. He contends that evangelical ideas provided the theological underpinnings for radical antislavery sentiment in both areas. While Finney's perfectionist doctrines provided the ideological base for western abolitionism, Garrison and his followers were strongly influenced by the New England evangelicals, Lyman

1 Brooks, "Massachusetts Anti-Slavery Society," *The Journal of Negro History*, XXX (July, 1945), 311–330; Zorn, "The New England Anti-Slavery Society: Pioneer Abolition Organization," *ibid.*, XLII (1957), 157–176.

2 Nye, *William Lloyd Garrison and the Humanitarian Reformers* (Boston, 1955).

Beecher and Nathaniel Taylor, whose theology was quite similar to Finney's.

In marked contrast to Rhodes, Barnes, Dumond, and others, however, Thomas argues that the western movement was planned and organized by "transplanted New Englanders." According to him, earlier interpretations overemphasize the importance of personalities and geographical factors, as abolitionism was in fact a product and extension of New England culture. Equally important, Thomas explores in greater depth than Barnes or Dumond the connections between abolitionism and evangelical ideas. What does Thomas mean when he says that "problems of social and political reform were reduced in the evangelical equation to elements of personal morality?" How does this outlook account for the militancy of abolitionists, their refusal to compromise, their lack of a concrete reform program, and their identification of slavery with sin?

An entirely different approach from that in the previous selections is found in David Donald's essay: "Toward a Reconsideration of Abolitionists." He views evangelical ideas as a surface manifestation of abolitionist fervor, not a fundamental reason for its rise in the 1830s. Noting that other historians have also felt a need for "a social interpretation of reform," Donald maintains that abolitionist leadership was provided by a displaced social elite, the sons and daughters of old and socially prominent New England families who were victims of a "status revolution." With the rise of industrialism, economic and political leadership in the North was seized by the "merchant prince, the manufacturing tycoon, [and] the corporation lawyer." In Donald's view, abolitionists were trying not only to free the slave but also to reassert "the traditional values of their class at home."

Donald's leading critic, Robert A. Skotheim, questions first the validity of applying generalizations based on a study of abolitionist leaders to the movement as a whole. And what does Donald mean, Skotheim asks, when he states that his analysis confirms "the traditional identification of radical anti-slavery with New England"? Is he arguing that most abolitionists were born in New England? Or is he saying that New England was abolitionism's geographical center? Skotheim concludes that Donald has probed to new psychological and sociological depths by attempting to explain the origins of abolitionism in terms of a status revolution but that his interpretation is unclear on many points and does not "present the comparative evidence necessary to establish the thesis." What comparative evidence does Donald need, according to Skotheim, before he can make a valid judgment as to whether social background was a decisive factor in determining the composition of abolitionist leadership?

Are Skotheim's criticisms of Donald's article valid? Is Donald on solid ground in questioning interpretations that see the origin of abolition in evangelical revivalism?

Whether or not one finds Donald's social interpretation convincing, it does exemplify efforts made by a number of historians in recent years to employ the methods and insights of other academic disciplines—sociology, cultural anthropology, and social psychology—in analyzing the origins and character of American reform movements. George E. Mowry and Richard Hofstadter, for example, interpret the Progressives in much the same way that Donald views the abolitionists, while Ari A. Hoogenboom applies the status revolution thesis to civil service reformers of the 1870s and 1880s.[3] Martin B. Duberman in his article "The Abolitionists and Psychology," shares with Donald, Hofstadter, Hoogenboom, and others, the conviction that interdisciplinary methods can enlarge our understanding of reformers and reform movements. He finds, however, that historians have thus far oversimplified the problems involved in applying such methods to historical questions.

Taking issue with the status revolution thesis, as well as with interpretations that attribute stereotyped personality traits to *all* abolitionists, Duberman argues that we "know far too little" at present "why men do anything—let alone why they do something as specific as joining a reform movement—to assert as confidently as historians have, the motives of whole groups of men." Duberman concludes that we "may never know enough about the human psyche to achieve a comprehensive analysis" of the motivations behind abolitionism, but that "our best hope for increased understanding in this area" lies in the "researches of psychology." What new developments have occurred in the field of psychology, according to Duberman, that now demand the attention of historians?

Historians disagree not only on the origins, geographical center, leadership, and motivating impulses of abolitionism. They are divided also on another aspect of the movement: the influence of British abolitionists on their American counterparts.

It should be pointed out that Gilbert H. Barnes was one of the first historians to recognize the importance of connections between British and American humanitarian reform movements, and his contention that the evangelical doctrine of "immediatism" was of British origin is expressed in the selection from his writings discussed above. For purposes of debate in this book, however, a passage from Frank Thistlethwaite's study, *The Anglo-American Connection in the Early Nineteenth Century* (1959), illustrates the view that American abolitionists were largely indebted to Britons for their methods and ideas. Like Barnes, Thistlethwaite maintains that the doctrine of immediatism was of British origin and that American tactics and methods of organization were patterned after British models. He points out, however,

---

3 Mowry, *The California Progressives* (Berkeley, 1951); Hofstadter, *The Age of Reform: from Bryan to F.D.R.* (New York, 1956); and Hoogenboom, *Outlawing the Spoils; a History of the Civil Service Reform Movement, 1865–1883* (Urbana, Ill., 1961).

that after a decade of active Anglo-American cooperation, British participation in the American movement gradually declined. Why, according to Thistlethwaite, were American abolitionists anxious to have British support? Why was the year 1840 "the highwater mark of Anglo-American agitation?" And what results—positive and negative—did Anglo-American cooperation achieve?

In the next selection Thomas F. Harwood analyzes the importance of British influence from a slightly different perspective. Unlike Barnes and Thistlethwaite, Harwood focuses attention on direct pressures exerted by British evangelical abolitionists on American churches during the 1830s. He asserts that although historians have recognized that schisms in American churches "helped to bring on secession and war," they have not fully appreciated the importance of British influences in producing these divisions. For example, he points out that a majority of both American Baptists and Methodists "resentfully rejected" British interference, but that the end result of British pressure was "increased dissension within each church and a notable increase in antislavery strength among Northern members." Although Harwood, in contrast to Barnes and Thistlethwaite, does not suggest that the United States was virtually "a British province" in moral and humanitarian affairs, the selections by these three writers taken together leave the impression that British influence permeated all aspects of the American abolitionist crusade.

David Brion Davis disagrees with this point of view, especially with the idea that the doctrine of immediatism evolved solely from British antislavery thought and experience. The "principle of immediatism," Davis maintains "had had a long and parallel development" in both the United States and Great Britain. If Americans "modeled their new societies and techniques on British examples," they were by no means dependent upon British reformers for their ideas. How does Davis account for "the striking coincidence that both the British and American antislavery movements had come to a crucial turning point by 1830?" And why does he say that immediatism "was at once a logical culmination of the antislavery movement and a token of a major shift in intellectual history"?

Up to this point, debate has revolved around questions relating to the origin and leadership of abolitionism, and the nature and extent of British influences on it. The focus of the book now shifts to still another controversial area of debate: the effects of abolitionism on the sectional crisis of the 1840s and 1850s.

A selection by Avery O. Craven, a leading "revisionist" historian who began writing in the late 1930s, opens debate on this question. The abolitionists, Craven asserts, were irresponsible fanatics who bear the responsibility for the secession of the South and the outbreak of war in 1861. By their unceasing opposition to "sin" and their unyielding attacks on the morals of slaveholders, the abolitionists succeeded only in convincing most Northerners that the South was a dangerous "slave power" bent on destroying the American dream. As a result, they created a psychological climate, North and South, where fear, hatred, and hysteria rather than reason prevailed. Civil War, Craven concludes, "was then in the making."

Why does Craven argue that the moral aggression abolitionists directed toward slaveholders stemmed from "resentments and fears born out of local conditions" rather than irreconcilable moral differences between North and South? And why does he maintain that Garrison's life "would probably have been spent in protesting even if slavery had never existed"?

C. Vann Woodward, whose conclusions are similar to Craven's, approaches the problem from a slightly different angle. He considers the reactions of Northern abolitionists to, and the results of, John Brown's raid on Harpers Ferry in 1859.

Up to the time of Brown's raid, Woodward states, most abolitionists had been "solemnly committed" to the use of nonviolent means to destroy slavery. The attack on Harpers Ferry, however, captured the imagination of most Northern intellectuals, and they began to idealize Brown "as a symbol of the moral order and social purpose of the Northern cause." As a result, the abolitionists began "to lose sight of their differences" with Brown "over the point of means and ended by totally compromising their creed of nonviolence." As time passed, the passions aroused by the raid deepened "into a pathological condition of mind" which destroyed the influence of moderates in both sections of the country. Thus, the "crisis of Harpers Ferry, a crisis of means, not of ends," proved to be the turning point of sectional conflict. "Paranoia continued to induce counterparanoia," Woodward concludes, "each antagonist infecting the other reciprocally, until the vicious spiral ended in war."

Woodward points out, however, that "the risk one runs in describing the reaction to Harpers Ferry is the risk of attributing to that event tendencies long manifest." What factors besides the abolitionist attack does Woodward cite in explaining why the South had long been "a society in the grips of an insecurity complex?" What conclusions does he draw from the fact that John Brown's raid, quite apart from the abolitionists' reaction to it, was "a blow at the most sensitive area of Southern consciousness"?

Russell B. Nye, in the next selection, takes issue with Craven's views on the existence of a slave power conspiracy, and, by implication at least, questions the relevancy of Woodward's criticisms of the means abolitionists used to achieve their ends.

Were the abolitionists on solid ground, Nye asks, in accusing slaveholders of organizing a secret conspiracy to extend slavery to the territories and free states, to destroy the civil liberties of free white men, to "control the policies of the Federal government, and [to] complete the formation of a nationwide ruling aristocracy based on a slave economy"? In a strict sense, no, Nye answers. But, he continues, "there was unity of belief among Southerners that slavery was a good system" and "the South was willing to infringe upon basic civil and personal rights, free speech, free thought, and constitutional liberty" in order to preserve and extend it. Therefore, the abolitionists cannot be dismissed as deluded or misguided fanatics who created a psychological climate that generated a needless war. Garrison, Phillips, Birney, and others were nor far wrong, Nye concludes, in believing that the slave power seriously jeopardized American ideals of freedom and democracy.

Thus, Nye looks upon the abolitionists as farsighted realists who awakened the American people to the dangers of slavery. Does this mean, then, that Nye regards the Civil War as an irrepressible conflict caused by irreconcilable moral, political, and economic differences that divided North and South? And is he arguing, in effect, that ends justify means in a righteous cause? The reader will have to decide these questions for himself, as he must in these two instances make implicit judgments rather than explicit analyses as to the full meaning of Nye's thesis.

A selection by Stanley Elkins, which takes issue with the views expressed by Craven, Woodward, and Nye, closes debate in this book. It is clear that war came in 1861, Elkins begins, because of the "estrangement of North and South over slavery." But did the urgency of the slavery question make war inevitable? Was the Civil War an unavoidable conflict between the forces of slavery and freedom as some historians have charged? Elkins answers, no. Was it a result of fear, hatred, and hysteria aroused by the extreme doctrines of abolitionists, as still others have asserted? Again Elkins answers in the negative. "Moderation," he contends, "was not really an alternative" to militant abolitionism. A healthy society needs, indeed must have, its moral passion and fanaticism. If this is true, what fatal flaw existed in American society to prevent a peaceable transition from slavery to freedom? Elkins believes that the anti-institutional character of American society was the real difficulty, not antislavery radicalism or proslavery extremism. In Elkins' view, how could the existence of strong national institutions in antebellum days have prevented war?

In reading the evaluations by Craven, Woodward, Nye, and Elkins on the effects of abolitionism on the sectional crisis, it must be remembered that they were not written in a social or political vacuum. A number of factors—education, social background, and the spirit of the times in which he lives as well as available evidence and the ability to analyze that evidence—influence a historian's outlook on a given subject.

Craven began writing during the 1930s, a decade during which the United States, disillusioned by Wilsonian idealism and the results of the World War I, reverted unrealistically to its traditional policy of nonintervention in world affairs. Nye's article, on the other hand, appeared at the end of the World War II. The Allied victory over fascism not only confirmed the belief of millions of Americans in the superiority of democratic ideals but convinced them, as never before, that democratic principles must be defended against aggression—by war if necessary. Quite clearly, the ideas expressed by Craven and Nye reflect to a degree the spirit of the times in which they were conceived. The same holds true for the ideas expressed by Woodward and Elkins, whose writings reveal, in part, a concern with the political and military realities of the Cold War—especially the necessity for inducing controlled change in a thermonuclear age.[4]

Does this necessarily mean that the ideas expressed by Craven, Woodward, Nye, and Elkins on the role played by abolitionism in the sectional crisis of the 1840s and 1850s are invalid? It is true, of course, that contemporary pressures sometimes prompt dubious historical analogies. But it is also true that the added perspective of time and experience can enhance our knowledge and understanding of the past.

While definitive answers to many of the questions raised here have not yet appeared—indeed, may never appear—historians have greatly increased our knowledge of the social and intellectual forces that helped to divide the nation during the antebellum period. It is the task of the reader to determine which interpretations in these pages have more validity than others and why. He can do so only if he attempts to answer for himself fundamental questions about the origin and motivating impulses of abolitionism, its significance, its effects—and, more important perhaps, about the nature and meaning of the concept we call history.

---

[4] A comprehensive discussion of factors that have influenced twentieth-century historical writing on the Civil War era is found in Thomas J. Pressly, *Americans Interpret Their Civil War* (Princeton, N.J., 1954). See also: Robert A. Skotheim, "The Writing of American Histories of Ideas: Two Traditions in the XXth Century," *Journal of the History of Ideas,* XXV (April–June, 1964), 257–278.

To his followers, William Lloyd Garrison appeared a man of heroic stature, a prophet anointed by God who organized and led the abolitionist crusade against slavery. This selection by JAMES FORD RHODES (1848–1927), a leading historian of his day, is essentially a restatement of the traditional Garrisonian interpretation of the movement.*

Garrison and the Abolitionists

William Lloyd Garrison began the abolitionist movement by the establishment of the *Liberator*[1] at Boston, January 1st, 1831. Although he had for several years been advocating anti-slavery ideas, his denunciations of slavery had attracted as little attention at the national capital as Paul's preaching excited in the palace of the Caesars. . . .

More than forty years had now passed since the establishment of the government. The hopes of its founders had not been realized, for the number of slaves was fast increasing, slavery had waxed strong and had become a source of great political and social power. While optimists, looking for a sign from heaven and a miracle, hoped that, by some occult process, the slaves would be freed voluntarily by the next generation, the abolitionists believed that reform from within the system could not be expected, but that its destruction must come from influences from the outside. The vital point was to convince the Northern people that slavery was a concern of theirs; that as long as it existed in the country without protest on their part, they were partners in the evil; and although debarred from legislative interference with the system, that was no reason why they should not think right on the subject, and bear testimony without ceasing against its hateful character.

[1] Garrison's newspaper (weekly). It was published until 1865.—*Ed.*

* From James Ford Rhodes, *History of the United States from the Compromise of 1850,* vol. 1 (New York: MacMillan and Co., 1906) pp. 53–63. Reprinted without footnotes.

The apostle who had especial fitness for the work, and who now came forward to embody this feeling and rouse the national conscience from the stupor of great material prosperity, was Garrison. Adopting the Stoic maxim, "My country is the world," he added its corollary, "My countrymen are all mankind," and with the change of *my* to *our* he made it the motto of the *Liberator*. In his salutatory address he said: "I shall strenuously contend for the immediate enfranchisement of our slave population. . . . I will be as harsh as truth and as uncompromising as justice. . . . I am in earnest—I will not equivocate—I will not excuse—I will not retreat a single inch—and I will be heard." In one of the succeeding issues he said: "Everybody is opposed to slavery, O, yes! there is an abundance of philanthropy among us. . . . I take it for granted slavery *is* a crime—a damning crime; therefore, my efforts shall be directed to the exposure of those who practice it." Soon the *Liberator* appeared with a pictorial heading that displayed the national capitol, floating from whose dome was a flag inscribed "Liberty"; in the foreground is seen a negro, flogged at a whipping-post, and the misery of a slave auction. The journal began in poverty; but in the course of the first year the subscription list reached five hundred. Garrison wrote the leading articles and then assisted to set them up in type and did other work of the printer.

In August of this year (1831) occurred the Nat Turner insurrection in Virginia, which seemed to many Southerners a legitimate fruit of the bold teaching of Garrison, although there was indeed between the two events no real connection. But this negro rising struck terror through the South and destroyed calm reason. . . . The massacre began at night and continued for forty-eight hours; women and children were not spared, and before the bloody work was checked sixty-one whites were victims of negro ferocity. The retribution was terrible. Negroes were shot, hanged, tortured, and burned to death, and all on whom suspicion lighted met a cruel fate. In Southampton County, the scene of the insurrection, there was a reign of terror, and alarm spread throughout the slave States.

This event, and the thought that it might be the precursor of others of the same kind, account for much of the Southern rage directed against Garrison and his crusade. Nor, when we reflect on the sparsely settled country, the wide distance between plantations—conditions that made a negro insurrection possible—and when we consider what it was for planters to have hanging over their heads the horrors of a servile war, will it seem surprising that judicial poise of temper was impossible when Southerners discussed the work of Garrison. They regarded it as an incitement for their slaves to revolt. But they did injustice to Garrison, for Nat Turner had never seen a copy of the *Liberator*, and the paper had not a single subscriber south of the Potomac. Nor did Garrison ever send a pamphlet or paper to any slave, nor advocate the right of physical resistance on the part of the oppressed. He was a non-resistant, and did not believe that force should be used to overturn legal authority, even when unjustly and oppressively exercised. The assertion that slavery is a damning crime is one thing; the actual incitement of slaves to insurrection is another. The distinction between the two was not appreciated at the South. Stringent laws were made against the circulation of the *Liberator*, and vigilance committees sent their warnings to any who were supposed to have a part in spreading its doctrines. In North Carolina Garrison was indicted for a felony, and the legislature of Georgia offered a reward of five thousand dollars for the arrest and conviction of the editor or publisher. One voice went abroad from public officials, popular meetings, and from the press of the South, demanding that the governor of Massachusetts or the mayor of Boston should suppress the "infernal *Liberator.*" . . .

Meanwhile Garrison and his little band continued the uphill work of proselyting at the North, and especially in Boston. Merchants, manufacturers, and capitalists were against the movement, for trade with the South was important, and they regarded the propagation of abolition sentiments as injurious to the commercial interests of Boston. Good society turned the back upon the abolitionists. Garrison had no college education to recommend him to an aristocracy based partly upon wealth and partly upon culture. The churches were bitterly opposed to the movement. Oliver Johnson, one of the early disciples of Garrison, relates that several times his efforts were in vain to persuade some one among a dozen white clergymen of Boston to open an anti-slavery meeting with prayer, and he was in each case forced at last to accept the services of a negro preacher from "Negro Hill." The position of the church was well expressed by a noted clergyman, who attributed the sin of slavery to a past generation, and assigned the duty of emancipation to future generations. The abolitionists, however, gradually gained ground. The year 1833 was for them one of grateful memory. Then, at Philadelphia, the American Anti-Slavery Society was organized by delegates who made up in enthu-

siasm what they lacked in numbers. The Declaration of Sentiments, drawn up by Garrison, was a paper worthy of the earnest and intelligent people who were its signers. It referred to the immortal Declaration adopted in the same city fifty-seven years before, and, as the strongest abolition argument that could be made, quoted the phrase "that all men are created equal; that they are endowed by their Creator with certain inalienable rights; that among these are life, liberty, and the pursuit of happiness." It denounced slavery in vigorous terms, yet conceded that Congress had no right to interfere with it in the States; and while condemning the employment of material force in any way to promote abolition, the signers pledged themselves to use moral means, so far as lay in their power, to overthrow the execrable system of slavery. This was not an inflammatory and seditious appeal; the delegates were men of good character, pure morals, and were law-abiding citizens; yet it was necessary for the police to guard the convention hall against threatened mob violence. The meeting was regarded by all Southern people, and by nearly all at the North, in much the same way as we should now look upon an assemblage of anarchists.

This year (1833) is also noteworthy as furnishing a fresh argument for the abolitionists. The British Parliament, influenced by a long course of agitation, emancipated the negro slaves in the West Indian colonies, so that henceforward freedom was the rule in all the vast colonial possessions of England, as it had been for years in the parent state.

At the same time, ambitious Southern politicians began to turn to their own advantage the anti-slavery agitation at the North. This did not escape the keen observation of [James] Madison, who, though well stricken in years, was able to detect, from his country retreat, the reason of various moves in the political sphere of his native state, which had for their aim to make a unit of Southern opinion on the slavery question. "It is painful," wrote Madison to [Henry] Clay in June, 1833, "to observe the unceasing efforts to alarm the South by imputations against the North of unconstitutional designs on the subject of the slaves." In a letter written more than a year later, he said that one could see from the Virginia newspapers and the proceedings of public meetings that aspiring popular leaders were inculcating the "impression of a permanent incompatibility of interests between the South and the North."

Excitement about the abolition movement characterized the year 1835. Numerous public meetings and the press of the South demanded almost with one voice that the abolitionists must be put down or they would destroy the Union. The suspension of commercial intercourse with the North was even suggested. The Charleston post-office was forcibly entered and a large number of tracts and papers sent there by the American Anti-Slavery Society[2] were seized; the next night these papers and effigies of Garrison and other abolitionists were burned in the presence of a large number of spectators. On a false alarm of a pro-

2 The national society of the abolitionists, organized at Philadelphia in 1833. Throughout the 1830s the society carried out an ambitious program which included the establishment of an agency system designed to convert the nation to the idea of "immediate repentance from the sin of slavery" and a petition campaign demanding that Congress abolish slavery in the District of Columbia. As a result of decentralizing forces inherent in the movement from its inception and as a result of a schism in abolitionist ranks, by 1840 the national society ceased to exist except in name.—*Ed.*

jected slave rising in Mississippi, several white men and negroes were hanged by vigilance committees. The wrath of the Southern people against the abolitionists was reflected at the North, and the feeling grew that the imputation of abolition ideas to the whole Northern community must be repelled. As the *Liberator* could not be suppressed, nor anti-slavery meetings prohibited by law, recourse was had to mob violence. Attacks upon abolitionists had previously been common, and this sort of warfare culminated in the year 1835. A ferocious anti-negro riot took place in Philadelphia. Rev. Samuel May, a devoted abolitionist and adherent of Garrison, was mobbed at Haverhill, Mass., the home of [John Greenleaf] Whittier, and five times afterwards at different places in Vermont. A disgraceful anti-slavery riot occurred at Utica, N.Y. In Boston, on the same day, a mob, variously estimated at from two thousand to five thousand, including many gentlemen of property and influence, broke up a meeting of the Boston Female Anti-Slavery Society. Garrison, one of the men against whom the mob directed its fury, had escaped from the hall in which the ladies were assembled, but was seized and dragged bareheaded through the streets, subjected to indignity and insult, and his life was threatened. The mayor and police finally rescued him from the hands of the rioters, and put him in jail as a protection against further violence.

Yet the work of converting and creating Northern sentiment went on. In spite of misrepresentation, obloquy, and derision, the abolitionists continued to apply moral ideas and Christian principles to the institution of slavery. The teachings of Christ and the Apostles actuated this crusade, and its latent power was great. If one looks for its results merely to the numbers of congressmen chosen by the abolitionists, to the vote received by presidential candidates distinctively theirs, or even to the number of members enrolled in the anti-slavery societies, only a faint idea of the force of the movement will be gained. The influence of the *Liberator* cannot be measured by its subscribers, any more than the French revolutionists of 1789 can be reckoned as of no greater number than the readers of "The Social Contract." If Rousseau had never lived, said Napoleon, there would have been no French Revolution. It would be historical dogmatism to say that if Garrison had not lived, the Republicans would not have succeeded in 1860. But if we wish to estimate correctly the influence of Garrison and his disciples, we must not stop with the enumeration of their avowed adherents. We must bear in mind the impelling power of their positive dogmas, and of their never-ceasing inculcation on those who were already voters and on thinking youths who were to become voters, and who, in their turn, prevailed upon others. We must picture to ourselves this process of argument, of discussion, of persuasion, going on for twenty-five years, with an ever-increasing momentum, and we cannot resist the conviction that this anti-slavery agitation had its part, and a great part too, in the first election of Lincoln. It was due to Garrison and his associates that slavery became a topic of discussion at every Northern fireside. Those who had heard the new doctrine gladly tried to convince their family and their friends; those who were half convinced wished to vanquish their doubts or have put to rest the rising suspicion that they

were partners in a great wrong; those who stubbornly refused to listen could not fail to feel that a new force had made its appearance, with which a reckoning must be made. Slavery could not bear examination. To describe it was to condemn it. There was a certain fitness, therefore, in the demand of the Southerners that the discussion of slavery in any shape should be no longer permitted at the North.

But in what a state of turpitude the North would have been if it had not bred abolitionists! If the abolitionists had not prepared the way, how would the political rising of 1854–60 against the slave power have been possible? It is true that many ardent Republicans who voted for Lincoln would have repudiated the notion that they were in any way influenced by the arguments of Garrison and his associates. And it is equally true that in 1835 the average Northern man satisfied himself by thinking slavery in the abstract a great evil, but that, as it existed in the South, it was none of his concern; he thought that "God hath made of one blood all nations of men" a good doctrine to be preached on Sunday, and "all men are created equal" a fit principle to be proclaimed on the Fourth of July; but he did not believe that these sentiments should be applied to the social condition of the South. But that was exactly the ground on which the abolitionists planted themselves, and, by stirring the national conscience, they made possible the formation of a political party whose cardinal principle was opposition to the extension of slavery, and whose reason for existence lay in the belief of its adherents that slavery in the South was wrong.

The traditional Garrisonian interpretation of abolitionism was not seriously challenged until 1933 when GILBERT H. BARNES (1889–1945) published his seminal study, *The Antislavery Impulse, 1830–1844.* According to Barnes, abolitionism was indeed a religious crusade, but it was not centered in New England under Garrison's leadership. Rather, it originated with the evangelical revivals of Charles Grandison Finney in the west—western New York, western Pennsylvania, and Ohio where tens of thousands rejected the tenets of orthodox Calvinism and dedicated their lives to the moral regeneration of all mankind.*

The Western Revival Origins

Some years ago [I] . . . began a study of the orgins of the antislavery movement. The orthodox account soon proved inapplicable, for in the records no link appeared between the New England agitation inspired by Garrison and his *Liberator,* and the New York movement which created the American Anti-Slavery Society. The problem then arose: if the influence of New England was not paramount in national antislavery beginnings, what was? The solution could be reached only by tracing to its origins each antislavery activity which in later years made up the national movement.

The American Anti-Slavery Society, it soon appeared, was conceived by its originators as the continuance of a chain of benevolent societies which had been founded during the two preceding decades and which by 1830 were well ramified through the nation. Their purpose was to promote Sunday-schools, missions, Sabbath observance, temperance, and similar agencies and excellences. Acting for no single denomination, they were nevertheless religious associations, working in the interest of interdenominational benevolence. They constituted what was called the benevolent system.

Though operating in the name of interchurch unity, the benevolent system

* From the introduction to the *Letters of Theodore Dwight Weld, Angelina Grimké Weld, and Sarah Grimké, 1822–1844,* edited by Gilbert H. Barnes and Dwight L. Dumond, vol. I, pp. V–XIX. Copyright, 1934, The American Historical Association. Reprinted by permission of Appleton-Century-Crofts. This introduction, written by Barnes, is a summary of the major conclusions contained in *The Antislavery Impulse, 1830–1844* (New York, 1933).

was controlled through a series of inter-locking directorates by a small number of Presbyterian and Congregational ministers and laymen. Among the latter the names of two wealthy merchants of New York, Arthur and Lewis Tappan, were the most prominent. . . .

In 1830 the benevolence of these brothers received fresh impetus. That year the famous Presbyterian revivalist, Charles Grandison Finney, invaded New York City, carrying thither the great revival which he had begun in western New York five years before. Inspired by his preaching, the Tappans initiated benevolent movements of their own. They provided a widespread system of churches for the poor of New York and secured a large downtown auditorium, Chatham Street Chapel, to be used both as an assembly hall for the annual con-ventions of the benevolent societies and as a church for New York's floating population. For pastor of this church the Tappans engaged the revivalist himself. They also founded a weekly, the *New York Evangelist,* to support Finney's views and extend his Great Revival throughout the nation.

Other benevolent initiatives inspired by Finney's influence were not so for-tunate. . . . [A] prominent failure was Arthur Tappan's attempt to reform the prostitutes of New York City. On the model of an English prototype, he or-ganized the American Magdalen Society, which founded an "Asylum for Females Who Have Deviated from the Paths of Virtue." Experience proved that the asy-lum did not produce "fruits of repent-ance" among the inmates, and it was abandoned. . . .

The use of an English model for the Magdalen Society was symptomatic. In moral even more than in literary affairs,

this country was still a British province, and British precedent was the highest authority throughout the benevolent sys-tem. Successful reforms in England were eagerly imitated on this side of the water, and the annual admonitions which corresponding sects and societies in England sent to their American brethren were for the most part faith-fully observed.

Toward the close of 1830 a new prec-edent was set for the benevolent system. The famous debate in Parliament on slavery in the West Indies impressed American philanthropists with the sig-nificance of the antislavery movement in Great Britain and fixed their attention upon the British Anti-Slavery Society. "Let us imitate our British brethren," said the *New York Evangelist,* "and open the floodgates of light on this dark sub-ject." In June of 1831 the Tappans called a conference of reformers, which pro-jected an "American National Anti-Slavery Society" after the British model, but "on a new and extensive plan." . . . On second thought, however, the Tap-pans decided to postpone the organiza-tion of the new society until emancipa-tion in the West Indies had become a published triumph. Meanwhile the con-ference of reformers—known among their contemporaries as "the New York Com-mittee"—labored . . . to prepare the way for national organization.

In the spring of 1833, when the West Indian emancipation bill was presented to Parliament, the New York Committee again proposed a national convention, to meet at Philadelphia, where the old Pennsylvania Society for the Abolition of Slavery had promised to lend facilita-tion. A date was set, October twenty-fifth, late enough to take advantage of the news of British emancipation. . . . But fierce opposition to an antislavery convention developed in Philadelphia, and the Pennsylvania Society for the Abolition of Slavery concluded that the time was not yet ripe for the national project. The New York Committee therefore postponed the date of the convention to 1834, fixing it to coincide with the annual meetings of the benevolent societies which were held in New York each May.

For reasons of his own, however, William Lloyd Garrison demanded a meeting in the current year of 1833. Though he had previously had no part in the plans of the New York Committee, his prestige among American abolitionists had recently been so enlarged by a visit to the abolitionists of Great Britain that his wishes could not be disregarded. . . . Preparations were hastily made, and a convention met at Philadelphia on December 5, 1833, with only a handful of delegates in attendance. This convention founded the American Anti-Slavery Society.

The first year of the new society's career produced little but hostility. In order to identify their movement with the triumphant British cause, the New York leaders felt obliged to adopt the British motto of immediate emancipation. In spite of their interpretation of this as meaning merely that the process of emancipation should have an immediate beginning—"immediate emancipation, gradually accomplished"—the general public understood their maxim as literal immediatism. . . . Naturally, the public judged the entire movement by the motto and not by the explanation; for as Channing, the New England liberal, remarked, however carefully they might "explain the word immediate so as to make it innocuous . . . it is a fatal mistake for a party to choose a watch word which almost certainly conveys a wrong sense and needs explanation."

Another handicap to the new society was the unfortunate repute of William Lloyd Garrison. . . . This repute by 1834 was nation-wide; but though it was based upon his editorial work in the *Liberator,* it was not the result of successful propaganda among his subscribers. For several years after its beginning, in 1831, the number of white subscribers to the *Liberator* was inconsiderable; and though the free Negroes of the Northern cities supported it faithfully, their public influence at that time was negligible. The reputation of the *Liberator* was made by its enemies and not by its subscribers.

According to the journalistic practice of the day, the *Liberator* was mailed to an exchange list of more than a hundred periodicals throughout the country. Most of those in the North ignored the paper; but Southern editors, with slaveholding constituencies already "in a state of phrensy" over the approach of emancipation in the West Indies, quoted it with enthusiasm. Garrison's editorial style was supremely quotable, but its content was made up of "rancorous denunciations and brawling, ferocious abuse." This evoked a furor of counter-attack, which so magnified Garrison's importance that his name became the very symbol of abolitionism. Though he had not been an initiator of the American Anti-Slavery Society and though he was never an important office-holder in it, his mere participation skewed the plans of the New York Committee by giving to the whole movement a seeming temper of rampant fanaticism. He was continually called the father of the society, and the *Liberator* was popularly considered its organ. Over the entire agitation his name cast "a vague and indefinite odium" which hampered its growth from the beginning.

Burdened with the epithet of "Garrisonism" and crippled by its misunderstood motto of immediatism, the society made small progress among the antislavery public of the North. Even in those communities where the hatred of slavery was most pervading and most intense, the society's agents usually encountered "a demonstration of popular indignation"; and with one or two exceptions, the agents of these early years had neither the fortitude nor the eloquence to subdue this hostility. . . . The pamphlet agitation fared little better. The motto of immediatism was so hard to explain and so likely to be misunderstood that the written word proved a poor medium for propaganda. . . . Even when the harmlessness of the motto was recognized, antislavery tracts provoked controversy. If the immediate abolition of slavery did not mean immediate freedom for the slave, what did it mean? If it involved some form of constraint "suitable to the freedman's condition," then it meant simply "the substitution of one type of slavery for another"—the condition of slavery under another name. On the other hand, if abolitionists meant by "immediate emancipation" a progressive loosening of the bonds of slavery, then they were *"gradualists* in fact though immediatists in language, liable to all the absurdity of immediate emancipation—fifty years hence." Inevitably the pamphlet controversy led to confusion.

Early in 1835, as the first year of agitation came to a close, leading abolitionists were admitting among themselves that "matters were tending to a disastrous result." Throughout the East the antislavery public was still indifferent or even hostile to the immediatist demand. Agitation by agents was almost at a standstill; and the pamphlet propaganda, barred from the South by the postal authorities, was evoking elsewhere little but antagonism and resentment. However, in the West at the same time, there was in preparation a tool for agitation which gave new hope. At Lane Seminary in Cincinnati the year before, a debate on slavery and its abolition had brought conviction to nearly all the students, Northerners and Southerners alike. Commissioned by the national society as agents for the West, these young men preached the antislavery cause as a revival in benevolence. . . . Most of them were from western New York, where they had been converted by Finney in the Great Revival; and they carried over into the antislavery cause the zeal of the Great Revival itself. Hostility they overcame by enduring it with steadfast meekness until the people would listen. They preached immediate emancipation; but in their hands it was more than the jesuitical "gradualism in a British cloak" of the New York philanthropists: it was an immediatism of repentance from sin. By making the sin of slavery "the standard to which the abolitionist is to rally," these agents made the antislavery cause "identical with religion; and men and women are exhorted by all they esteem holy, by all the high and exciting obligations of duty to man and God, . . . to join in the pious work of purging the sin of slavery from the land." In Ohio, Pennsylvania, and New York, and even in parts of distant New England, these agents from Lane Seminary precipitated another Great Revival, a revival in abolitionism.

By the spring of 1836 the success of

the "Lane rebels" had become so clear that the national society decided to abandon the pamphlet propaganda and concentrate all its resources on enlarging the group of abolition evangelists to the number of seventy, the number sent out in Bible times to convert the world to Christianity. . . . Before they began their work, these recruits were assembled at New York, where for weeks they received from the greatest of the Lane Seminary agents a pentecostal training in the gospel of abolitionism. Then they were sent out to convert the North, where they produced among the churches "a great concussion in the earth and heavens, portentous, we trust, to their passing away."

In 1836, the year that the Seventy began their labors, a fresh and special objective was presented to the antislavery cause. In the House of Representatives a rule was adopted denying a hearing to petitions for antislavery objects. Abolitionists denounced this rule as violating their constitutional right of petition, and the Northern public believed them. . . .

Indeed, before the passage of the rule against petitions, reformist opinion outside the circle of the Lane rebels' labors had little basis for anything but hostility. Convinced that the doctrine of the abolitionists was literal immediatism and that Garrison was their leader, even honest antislavery reformers had been unfriendly. Now, however, the movement stood for something more than "Garrisonism" and immediatism: it stood for the constitutional right of petition. Thousands joined the society, and thousands more, "inimical to the object of the petitioners," furthered the petition campaign with their signatures, "preferring that the object of the petitioners should be attained rather than that the sanctuary

of all our rights should be violated."

Circumstances in Congress favored the campaign. At the moment the Democrats controlled the House, and between them and the Whigs an intense partisan warfare was being waged. The Whig minority "was tyrannized over," complained a member, "and they were naturally in a refractory, restless and perturbed condition, and if they could not be heard orderly they would do so disorderly." To raise disorder no better device than abolition petitions could have been used. Northern Whigs presented them in duty to their constituents and demanded that they be received and read. When charged with obstructing needful business, they replied that they were fighting for the constitutional right of petition; and though an indignant Democratic member declared that "no man believes here that the right of petition is or ever has been in danger by the action of this House," there was sufficient public sentiment in the North to sustain the Whig position.

But though the campaign for the right of petition was primarily an instrument of obstruction, the incidental discussions of slavery which it permitted, occurring as they did on "the rostrum of the nation," were of great importance to the antislavery cause. . . . Realizing this, in 1837 the American Anti-Slavery Society planned a campaign to overwhelm Congress with petitions. Heretofore the antislavery organization had been too weak and decentralized to permit such a measure, but now the society was more than mere numbers. During the previous year the Seventy had been consolidating membership everywhere in the rural districts behind the cities, drawing together local organizations into new county societies, putting district leaders in touch with the central office, and inspiring old members and new alike with the spirit of the Great Revival. Thousands were now incipient revivalists in benevolence, ready "to make themselves useful in the highest degree. . . ."

Among these enthusiasts the society built its organization, the greatest non-political instrument for propaganda that had ever been achieved in the nation. District by district and county by county, leaders were designated to organize volunteer bands of workers. These leaders were supplied by the New York office with packages of blank petitions, together with minute directions as to their circulation and disposal. From the initial appointment of the leaders to the final count of signatures every step in the process was controlled by the New York headquarters. From that focus and from other points throughout the North the petitions were finally shipped in great bales to "safe men" in Congress, who presented them one by one on the floor of the House.

Abolitionists by the thousands volunteered to circulate the petitions; but they did not find it easy, because these petitions, like the rest of the abolition program, soon acquired the double stigma of "Garrisonism" and immediatism. . . .

For elucidation and instruction the volunteers turned to the national society. For the first time a demand for anti-slavery tracts in quantity reached the New York office. This demand, however, was not for the newspapers and short appeals, which had previously been the main reliance, but for solid treatises upon antislavery doctrine. To convince the pious, the American Anti-Slavery Society published *The Bible Against Slavery,* an exhaustive summary of the Lane Seminary agents' doctrine that slavery was a

sin. To sustain the case for abolition in the District, the society published *The Power of Congress over the District of Columbia,* which elaborated the municipal theory of slavery, the basis years later of Republican party doctrine. The lack of social menace in the abolition program was argued by *Emancipation in the West Indies;* and the horrors of slavery itself were exhibited in the greatest tract of them all, *Slavery As It Is,* the handbook of the movement for more than a decade.

Such solid works as these embodied the whole antislavery gospel. To a considerable extent they took the place of agents, especially in the area already canvassed. They were sold in unprecedented quantities. Indeed, in the first year of its publication, *Slavery As It Is* was said to be the best-selling book in the nation. The society's printed output reached unprecedented volume; but it was now largely a product of demand from the field, paid for by the localities, rather than of gratuitous distribution from the center. From these tracts, the volunteers to whom antislavery memorials were entrusted prepared themselves to convert their neighbors to the reasonableness of abolition itself, if conversion would secure signatures.

The shifting of the emphasis in propaganda from oratory to memorials worked a profound change in antislavery organization. Even more than the new tracts, the labors of local abolitionists with petitions reduced the need for agents; for their house-to-house visits in persuasive quest of signatures not only maintained the agitation but brought to bear "*a neighborhood influence*" upon the unconverted "for which nothing can be made a substitute . . . as information is thus carried where our editors and lec-

turers are utterly unable to penetrate."
As the number of volunteer workers increased, agents were withdrawn; and by
1840 the thousands of petition volunteers possessed the field.

Even more important was the localiz-
ing tendency of the petition campaign.
Once the volunteers had rightly learned
how to circulate petitions and send them
in, central control of their labors was
no longer necessary. Consequently, after
the first great campaign, in the spring of
1838, the State and national societies
gave over petition control to local agencies and retired from active leadership.
Thereafter petitions were printed in
blank on village presses, circulated in
the neighborhoods, and transmitted directly to John Quincy Adams or to
some other "safe" Congressman for presentation.

Still more a local matter was the movement to elect "safe men" to office. The
questioning of candidates for Congress
and for the State legislatures as to their
attitudes toward the right of petition,
abolition in the District of Columbia,
and similar matters was a business for
which outside aid was not helpful or
even desirable.

This spontaneous decentralization was
made the more complete by the financial
depression which followed the panic of
1837. In particular, the Tappan bankruptcy destroyed a main source of rev-
enue. Nevertheless, local contributions
for local measures continued to increase
almost everywhere, despite the depression; while support for the State and
national units fell away.

By the end of 1838 all of the larger
State societies had fallen apart; some
were bankrupt; and the American Anti-
Slavery Society was slowly starving to
death. The decline of their constituency

left the rulers of the society without
sufficient authority to keep radical minorities in the movement under control. The
Boston abolitionists and "third party"
champions in western New York made
trouble in the antislavery press; and the
New York executives, bankrupt and helpless, were unable to keep them in line.
Meanwhile, however, the antislavery
issue sharpened daily. It agitated lodges
and legislatures; it divided religious denominations. The subject "occupies and
absorbs the minds of nine-tenths of the
folks one meets," wrote a diarist. "All
other topics run into and are swallowed
up by this troubled reservoir of party
spirit and infuriated patriotism. What a
happy country to be so well looked after
by its citizens!"

By 1839 disorganization and controversy within the antislavery ranks had
made the national society "a stench in
the nostrils of the nation"; and many
abolitionists had come to believe that its
continued existence was a menace to the
cause. Apprehending this, John Quincy
Adams, now leader of the petition forces
in Congress and unofficial spokesman for
the petition volunteers, wrote a public
indictment of the American Anti-Slavery
Society. He declared that so long as it
represented the antislavery movement,
emancipation "in this Union, or even in
the District of Columbia, is as far beyond
the regions of possibility as any project
of the philosophers of Laputa."[1]

Adams's indictment provoked a frank
discussion in the antislavery press. With
only two exceptions, abolition editors
concluded that the usefulness of national
organization was ended. They advised
the society "to quietly dissolve itself" at
the next annual convention in 1840.

[1] Allusion to Jonathan Swift, *Gulliver's
Travels*, Book Three.—*Ed.*

Thereupon the New York leaders called a special meeting of the society, which came to the same conclusion; and a committee was appointed with power to liquidate the organization. The committee sold the society's property, paid its debts, and prepared it for extinction.

But the dissolution of the society thus arranged by its friends did not proceed according to plan. Garrison and the Boston abolitionists chartered a steamboat, transported "a large portion of the town of Lynn" to the annual meeting, and by their votes captured the convention and the society. However, all but the handful of Garrison's followers shortly withdrew, and the national organization ceased to exist in everything but name.

Meanwhile, in the field, the petition campaign approached its climax. Volunteers by the thousands bombarded their neighbors with antislavery arguments. Petitions by tens of thousands piled upon the desks of their State and national representatives. In 1840, the year that national antislavery organization ended in all but name, Adams noted in the House of Representatives "a greater number of petitions than at any former session."

It is clear that by 1840 the antislavery movement had shifted to the petition struggle, and its center was at Washington. Here the aged Adams conducted his unique agitation for the right of petition, and a little band of antislavery Whigs— Joshua Giddings from Ohio, William Slade from Vermont, Seth M. Gates from western New York, and a handful more— faithfully presented antislavery petitions and waged war for their reception. Before 1841 they conformed their tactics more or less faithfully to Whig party policy. They refrained from direct attacks on slavery, confining their warfare to oblique movements under cover of the petition campaign. But with the enlargement of the antislavery agitation wrought by the petition volunteers . . . they decided to break with Whig policy and begin an insurgent war upon slavery on the floor of the House.

Adams opened their campaign. On the pretext of a question of privilege, he made a bitter oration against "every slaveholder, slavetrader and slavebreeder on this floor" and in the nation. Whig leaders, fearful of the intersectional unity of their party, . . . proposed a resolution of censure against him; but Adams's prestige proved to be greater than party authority. The entire North, Whig as well as Democrat, rose up in defense of "Old Man Eloquent," and the frightened Whig chieftains tabled the resolution.

Joshua Giddings opened the second battle in the campaign with a series of powerful antislavery resolutions based upon what was called the *Creole* case. He was straightway censured by his Whig colleagues, without even being granted the right to speak in his own defense. He promptly resigned his seat and returned to his district in Ohio to stand for reëlection.

This campaign was one of the most important in party history. Indeed, political experts recognized at the time that in the question of Giddings's reëlection the entire issue of party regularity and party insurgency was joined. If the Whig party could secure his defeat, antislavery insurgency was doomed; but if they failed and he was reëlected, insurgency would receive its vindication. Whig leaders in Ohio as well as in Washington threw the whole weight of party interest against him, but their efforts were vain. For Giddings's district, by coincidence, was the very one in which the Lane Seminary agents had begun the abolition revival; and the issue there was not party regularity; it was the righteousness of the antislavery cause. Giddings was returned by a large majority—"the greatest triumph," a Southern spokesman told him, "achieved by a member of the House"— and the question of antislavery insurgency was thereby closed. . . .

Thereafter the insurgent group of Congressmen formed an antislavery bloc in Congress, which became the nucleus of a new movement in national affairs. Session by session their numbers grew, and upon each issue with an antislavery aspect they spoke with increasing authority for the abolition host. Inevitably they divided their party and the nation.

This, in brief outline, is the story which I found in contemporary documents. To me it seemed that the agitation was accomplished not so much by heroes of reform as by very numerous obscure persons, prompted by an impulse religious in character and evangelical in spirit, which began in the Great Revival in 1830, was translated for a time into antislavery organization, and then broadened into a Congressional movement against slavery and the South.

Still the impulse had its men of power. Among them the greatest figure from its earliest beginnings to its turning point in Congress was one hitherto unknown to me, Theodore Weld. In the council of reformers which met at New York in the spring of 1831 to organize an "American National Anti-Slavery Society . . . upon an enlarged and extensive plan," his was the moving spirit. The next year, on a journey in the West and South, he established centers of abolitionism which were later of vital importance. At Western Reserve College he advocated abolitionism among the faculty, and Elizur Wright, Jr., Beriah Green, and President Storrs

turned straightway to the task of converting the Western Reserve to the cause. At Huntsville, Alabama, he discussed with James G. Birney the wrongs of slavery, and Birney immediately abandoned a prosperous legal practice in order to begin his life of labor for the slaves. At St. Louis, Cincinnati, Cleveland, and elsewhere, Weld converted others of lesser fame to abolitionism.

On this journey Weld held a commission from the New York philanthropists to find a site for a theological seminary. He located it at Cincinnati, and through his wide acquaintance with young men who had been converted in the Great Revival (he had been Finney's most successful assistant) he supplied the bulk of the students. Among them, in 1834, he organized and conducted the great debate on slavery; and when the trustees ordered the discussion to cease, he led the students' hegira from that institution. These rebel students formed the group from which were chosen the antislavery agents who began the abolition revival. When the pamphlet propaganda failed and the movement faced disaster, their efforts saved the cause. "God thrust them out, full of philanthropy and zeal, to awake a slumbering nation," declared an abolitionist. H. B. Stanton, James Thome, Augustus Wattles, Hiram Wilson, Marius Robinson, Allan, Streeter, Dresser, Gould, Weed, and a score besides—their names make up a roll of heroes.

Weld's own antislavery agency probably accomplished more than those of all the rest combined. Theodore Smith, in his study of the Liberty and Free Soil parties in the Northwest,[2] came to the conclusion that Ohio abolitionism owed

[2] Theodore Clark Smith, *The Liberty and Free Soil Parties in the Northwest* (New York, 1897)—*Ed.*

more to Weld's labors than to any other single cause; but, if he had extended his study to western Pennsylvania and New York, he would have come to a similar conclusion there. The area of Weld's agency in these States and the regional chart of antislavery societies in the West of 1837 coincide.

. . . His antislavery meetings, usually eight evenings in succession, sometimes sixteen or even twenty, were, in form and spirit, like the "protracted meetings" of Finney's Great Revival. At their conclusion he would call upon converts to abolitionism to stand. Usually the whole audience would rise, not alone the restless reformers but the sober business and professional men of the community. He was especially powerful with lawyers: Joshua Giddings, Henry B. Stanton, Seth M. Gates, Clarke, Nixon, Andrews, and many others later prominent in national politics were converted by his preaching. Among Presbyterian ministers he wrought with even greater power. At the General Assembly of the Presbyterian Church, in Pittsburgh, his ministerial converts organized an antislavery lobby which, under his leadership, enlisted to the abolition cause "more than one-fourth part of the delegates to the assembly."

In the spring of 1836, when the American Anti-Slavery Society decided to abandon pamphleteering as a major measure and to increase the number of agents, it was Weld who with Whittier and Stanton selected the Seventy; and it was Weld again who took them in hand at their convention in New York. For weeks, "scarcely allowing time to eat or sleep," he imparted to them his antislavery lore and inspired them with his zeal.

After the agents' convention, his health impaired and his voice gone, Weld still labored for the cause. It was his hand that wrote the great tracts which embodied the antislavery doctrine—*The Bible Against Slavery, The Power of Congress,* and *Slavery As It Is.* Even the tract, *Emancipation in the West Indies,* though it bears the names of Thome and Kimball, is unmistakably in Weld's clear and emphatic style.

Finally, in Washington, at the turning point of the movement, when the antislavery Congressmen were hesitating between Whig party regularity and an insurgent war upon slavery in the House, it was Weld, lobbyist for abolition, who guided their decision, as Giddings's correspondence clearly shows.

So much contemporary newspapers, pamphlets, and manuscripts indicated. I was forced to the conclusion that, though Weld did not originate and dominate the antislavery agitation, as people a generation ago supposed William Lloyd Garrison to have done, still he was the movement's man of power, the greatest individual factor in its triumph.

The work of DWIGHT L. DUMOND (1895–   ), emeritus professor of American history at the University of Michigan, in many ways parallels that of Barnes. Like Barnes, Dumond emphasizes the impact of western evangelical revivalism in explaining the origins of abolitionism, and he minimizes Garrison's importance. However, Dumond stresses the importance also of other impulses in the rise of antislavery radicalism in the west. In this selection Dumond focuses attention on the contributions made by Southern "exiles" in providing leadership for the movement.*

Migrations to the Free States a Factor

Antislavery sentiment [in the South] was expressed in the early years [of the Republic] only by men who lived in states where the slave power was too weak to prevent it, or by men powerful enough —most of them slaveholders from Virginia —to defy the slave power, or by men who lived in the *nonslaveholding communities* of the South. Just as soon as, and wherever the slave power became consolidated, antislavery utterances were silenced. It was consolidated, it was militant, it was on the march, by the 1830's; and *far from reconstructing its defenses from a feeling of desperation and exasperation, it was reaching out to silence its critics everywhere and to expand its*

power to the whole of the continent. It moved from strength and a sense of power, not from fear and weakness.

One reason, indeed the primary reason, for this unwarranted sense of power— and, of course, it was unwarranted—was the fact that the South had lost its balance and sense of proportion. As the Black Belt developed and slavery and the power of the slaveholders began to dominate the lower South, liberals moved out. They went to the free states. They became the most outspoken critics of slavery, and they knew whereof they spoke. Most of them were slaveholders previous to their migration, or came from slaveholding families. They were exiles in a

* Reprinted from *Antislavery: the Crusade for Freedom in America* by Dwight L. Dumond by permission of The University of Michigan Press. © 1961 by The University of Michigan. Pp. 87–88, 90–95. Footnotes omitted by permission of the publisher.

very real sense, for some of them, certainly, would have been killed had they ventured back to the South.

The migration of these people was not a part of the westward movement. People moved west from the Carolinas, and Georgia, and Virginia, just as they moved west from New York, Pennsylvania, and New England. They moved southwest and northwest. We can identify many such. They moved for diverse reasons: to get away from the restraints and conventions of old, established communities, to find more elbow room, to get land or cheaper land. There is a voluminous literature on the subject, familiar to everyone. Some of these people were honest, hard-working people of all sorts from homestead farmers to carpenters and woodcutters who found intolerable the stigma on honest toil in the slave country. Some farmers moved because the entire economy was geared to the needs of slaveholding planters, and marketing and shipping became increasingly difficult as plantations developed. Some were paid high prices for their lands. Some were bitter because legislatures dominated by slaveholders, who could afford private instruction for their children, refused to build public schools.

Let us dwell a moment on this point of nonslaveholders' grievances. The legislature of North Carolina, for example, refused until 1840 to provide in any way for a system of public education. In consequence, the Census of 1850 showed 80,000 illiterate free persons in the state. One writer puts the figure at 71,150 persons over twenty-one years of age. The argument over schools and roads became so serious that it finally led to threats of violence. Benjamin Sherwood Hedrick, professor of chemistry at the University of North Carolina, said of migration

from that state: "Of my neighbors, friends and kindred, nearly one-half have left the State since I was old enough to remember. Many is the time I have stood by the loaded emigrant wagon and given the parting hand to those whose faces I was never to look upon again. They were going to seek homes in the free West, knowing, as they did, that free and slave labor could not both exist and prosper in the same community." Still more to the point was the statement of Henry Ruffner, president of Washington College (Lexington, Va.), in 1847. Saying that Virginia had lost by emigration 300,000 more persons than all of the old free states, he continued: "She has sent—or we should rather say, she has driven from her soil—at least one third of all the emigrants, who have gone from the old States to the new. More than another third have gone from the other old slave states. . . . These were generally industrious and enterprising white men, who found by sad experience, that a country of slaves was not the country for them. It is a truth, a certain truth, that slavery drives free laborers,—farmers, mechanics, and all, and some of the best of them too—out of the country, and fills their places with negroes."

All of this was part of the westward movement—very important in the slavery controversy as we shall see—but not in this particular aspect of it. The movement we are talking about was a distinct, easily recognizable, and clearly defined migration of people away from the slave power. These were men and women who simply refused to live in the *atmosphere* of slavery. They were cultivated men and women in the finest tradition of those who had preceded them in the contest: of Franklin, Rush, and Rice, for example. Fortunately, life loses meaning for our choicest souls unless they can help the underprivileged and oppressed. The mere sight of the victims of prejudice and greed, in slavery, was unbearable to these people. Honorable men and women, given to honest thinking, simply could not breathe in an atmosphere where they not only could do nothing about it, and say nothing about it, but were expected to condone and publicly approve it. The rapid rise of the slave power bore them down and drove them out.

Once out of the reach of the slave power, these people were free to speak and to write, which they did with telling effect. Some men who have written about the South and slavery have refused to recognize what they said as valid source materials. Others have looked casually at a few items and professed to have seen it all. Actually, it is our finest evidence as to what slavery really was, because these people had been slaveholders, had been reared in slave communities, had gone into exile rather than be silent about it, and were free to tell what they knew. They were relatively free from violence, they could find publishers and establish printing presses, and the public was willing to read and listen. Naturally, they became leaders in the antislavery movement. They would have been, had they been allowed to remain in the slave states. Among them were James Gillespie Birney, foremost exponent of constitutional theory and champion of civil rights; Edward Coles, governor of Illinois and staunch opponent of slavery expansion; Levi Coffin, "president" of the underground railroad; John Rankin, defender of the faith in one General Assembly of the Presbyterian Church after another; Angelina Grimké, champion of women's rights and coauthor of the greatest indictment of slavery ever written;

and a host of others of equal stature.

Preachers were among the first to feel the pressure for conformity, because there never was a more pronounced moral issue, and the slave power insisted it was and must remain a political question. Eventually, the Southern churches accepted that point of view, officially at least, but not until a good many incidents occurred. The Baptist David Barrow was one of these men. He was born in 1753 and preached in southern Virginia and northern North Carolina. In 1795 he founded the Portsmouth-Norfolk church and installed Jacob Bishop, a Negro, as pastor, with a mixed Negro-white congregation. He was subjected to much criticism and some violence, and moved in 1798, under strong pressure, to Kentucky. In Kentucky in 1805 he was expelled from the North District Association of Baptists because of his views on slavery, wrote his pamphlet *Involuntary, Unlimited, Perpetual, Absolute, Hereditary Slavery Examined on the Principles of Nature, Reason, Justice, Policy, and Scripture,* and served as president of the Kentucky Abolition Society for many years. He died in 1819.

David Rice was a Virginia Presbyterian and a graduate of Princeton. He was much older than Barrow, having been born in 1733, and having begun his ministry in 1767. He left Virginia in 1783 because of opposition to his antislavery principles and went to Kentucky, where he established the first grammar school in the West, helped to found Transylvania, and served as chairman of its board of trustees for many years. We are already familiar with his remarkable speech in the Kentucky Constitutional Convention. He afterward was active in the Kentucky Abolition Society, which failed to survive.

We are more familiar with the work of Barrow and Rice because they left us written records of their antislavery views, but there were others in this area. William Hickman, born in Virginia in 1747, settled near Lexington, Kentucky, in 1784 and became pastor of the Baptist Church at Forks of the Elkhorn. The Elkhorn Association censured him in 1805 saying "this Association judges it improper for ministers, churches, or associations, to meddle with emancipation from slavery or any other political subject, and as such, we advise ministers and churches to have nothing to do therewith in their religious capacities." Hickman threw the slaveholders out of his church, but was forced to resign. He returned later, obviously with an understanding to avoid the subject.

George Smith, born in Virginia in 1747 of Episcopalian parents, went to Kentucky as a Baptist preacher in 1804. His strong antislavery views made him exceedingly unpopular, but he preached until his death in 1820. Carter Tarrant, one of the earliest settlers in Logan County, Kentucky, came from Virginia and preached at the Hillsboro and Clear Creek churches. He and a member of his church, John Sutton, founded the first antislavery church in Woodford County. He died while serving as a chaplain in the Army in the War of 1812. Another antislavery church was founded at Bardstown by Joshua Carman, in 1796, but failed to survive.

Here was the record of honest, sincere frontier preachers who failed to gain more than a momentary hearing in their struggle against slavery, just as Rice had failed in the constitutional convention of the state. There was no central governing body of the Baptist churches to which they could carry an appeal. But over the long view, they did not fail, because other men were coming from the deep South to build on the foundations they had laid and this was soon to become a very important area of antislavery activity.

James Gilliland was born (1761) and reared in South Carolina. He was opposed to slavery, and, after graduating from Dickinson College, Pennsylvania, returned to South Carolina to preach in 1796. He was charged by twelve members of his congregation with political treason for preaching against slavery, and the Presbyterian Synod of the Carolinas, meeting at Morganton, November 3, 1796, decreed that he could not speak publicly for emancipation. He obeyed for a time, but moved to the greatest single mecca for emancipated slaves and ex-slave holders, Brown County, Ohio, in 1805. Here, he served as pastor of the Red Oak church for thirty-nine years, to a congregation of ex-slaveholders and other emigrants from the South. He was an uncompromising advocate of immediate emancipation and was second on the list of vice-presidents of the American Anti-Slavery Society when it was organized in 1833. He was affectionately known as Father Gilliland and founded churches at Ripley, Russellville, Decatur, and Georgetown.

There was born in Virginia in 1749 a most remarkable man, Samuel Doak, who graduated from Princeton in 1775 and was licensed to preach by the Presbytery of Hanover, Virginia. He married, moved to Fork Church, North Carolina (later Tennessee), and founded (1783) at Little Limestone, near Jonesboro, Martin Academy, with a charter from the state. He founded Washington College in 1795 and served as its president until 1818, at which time he founded, at New Bethel,

Tusculum Academy. He was opposed to slavery; freed his slaves and sent them to Brown County, Ohio; and trained a host of young preachers, nearly all of whom went to the Old Northwest. Among them were Gideon Blackburn, John Rankin, and David Nelson. Sometime in the 1820's, Doak moved to Ohio, where he died in 1830.

Doak's son-in-law was John Rankin, born in Tennessee, in 1793. He studied under Doak, later married his daughter, and was licensed to preach in 1817. He was a staunch opponent of slavery and active in the Kentucky Abolition Society while preaching at Carlisle in 1817–21. He then moved to Ripley, Ohio, where he served as pastor of the Presbyterian Church for forty-four years. He converted his home into a haven of refuge for fugitives crossing the river and was mobbed many times by irate Kentuckians. A series of his letters first published in 1823 and reprinted in book form as *Letters on American Slavery, Addressed to Mr. Thomas Rankin, Merchant at Middlebrook, Augusta County, Virginia* remains one of the twenty-five most important antislavery publications. He later served as a lecturer for the American Anti-Slavery Society, but his most important contribution was in the Presbyterian General Assemblies, where year after year he led the fight against slavery until the schism of 1837.

There came also to the Chillicothe Presbytery in early years, James H. Dickey, born in Virginia in 1780, and William Dickey, a native of South Carolina. James began his ministerial career as a missionary in Tennessee, but freed the slaves inherited by himself and his wife, and went to South Salem, Ohio, in 1810, where he became widely known for his antislavery work. William Dickey

moved with his family from South Carolina to Kentucky where he preached for seventeen years. He went to Ohio, organized a church at Bloomingsburg in 1818, and served as its pastor for forty years. Finally, there came from Pennsylvania by way of Kentucky, Samuel Crothers. He had intended to make Winchester, Kentucky, his home, but moved to Ross County, Ohio, where he preached from 1810 to 1820 and then went to Greenfield, where he organized the Paint Valley Abolition Society. Gilliland, Rankin, the two Dickeys, and Samuel Crothers made the Chillicothe Presbytery of Ohio an antislavery stronghold before 1820. Rankin quickly emerged as a national figure in the movement.

Another of the giants in the movement was Levi Coffin, born in North Carolina in 1789. He was of a family of Quakers, by instinct and tradition opposed to slavery. Opposition to his religious instruction of the slaves in the New Garden area led to his migration to Newport, Indiana, in 1826. Here he devoted as much time to aiding the fugitives as to business, helped three thousand slaves on their way to freedom, and ultimately became the most important figure in that exciting phase of antislavery work. He was in Cincinnati during the riotous forties and continued his aid to freedmen until long after the Civil War.

From the schools of Samuel Doak in Tennessee came a number of men. Gideon Blackburn was born in Virginia, in 1772. His family moved to Tennessee, where he attended Martin Academy. He was licensed to preach at twenty, founded a church at New Providence in 1792, and conducted a school for Cherokee children from 1804 to 1810. He became pastor of the Presbyterian church at Louisville in 1823, and president of Centre College at

Danville in 1827. He went to Illinois in 1833, assisted Elijah P. Lovejoy in organizing the Illinois Antislavery Society, and founded Blackburn College at Carlinville.

David Nelson, born in Tennessee in 1793, studied under Doak, served as a surgeon in the War of 1812, became pastor of the Presbyterian church in Danville in 1828, rose to national prominence as director of education for the church, freed his slaves in Kentucky and went to Palmyra, Missouri, as president of Marion College. He was driven from his pulpit and from the state for advocating compensated emancipation, and barely escaped with his life into Illinois.

Thomas Morris was born in Virginia in 1776. He was bitterly opposed to slavery and moved to Ohio in 1795, where he studied law at night while making a living, as a brickmaker, for a family of eleven children. He served in the Ohio legislature from 1806 to 1830, as chief justice of the state from 1830 to 1833, and as United States senator from 1833 to 1839. In the Senate he led the fight for the right of petition, fought Calhoun's resolutions of 1837, and delivered a masterful defense of civil rights in debate with Henry Clay. He was read out of his party and promptly joined in the political movement to abolish slavery.

Two Virginians of equal stature went to Illinois to escape slavery, and their combined efforts probably kept that state free. James Lemen settled at New Design in 1786, organized the first eight Baptist churches, all on an antislavery basis, diligently counteracted the many proslavery petitions sent to Congress while William Henry Harrison was governor of Indiana Territory, and organized "The Baptized Church of Christ, Friends of Humanity, on Cantine Creek," with a constitution "denying union and communion with all persons holding the doctrine of perpetual, involuntary, hereditary slavery." This close-knit organization gave tremendous weight to Lemen's work as a member of the first Constitutional Convention. "The church," it was said, "properly speaking, never entered politics, but presently, when it became strong, the members all formed what they called the 'Illinois Anti-Slavery League,' and it was this body that conducted the antislavery contest. It always kept one of its members and several of its friends in the territorial legislature, and five years before the constitutional election in 1818 it had fifty resident agents—men of like sympathies—in the several settlements throughout the territory quietly at work."

Edward Coles was born in Virginia in 1786, of wealthy, slaveholding parents. He was educated at Hampden-Sidney College and William and Mary College, served as private secretary to President Madison from 1809 to 1815, and went to Russia on a diplomatic mission in 1816. Coles made plans to free his slaves as early as 1815. In the spring of 1819 he took his slaves by boat to the West and gave them freedom and land upon which to start a new life. He immediately made common cause with the antislavery forces of Lemen's association, was elected governor in 1822 by a narrow margin, and was a tower of strength in preventing adoption of a new proslavery constitution.

Finally, there came into this area two stalwarts of the later movement: William T. Allan and James A. Thome. Allan was the son of the Presbyterian minister at Huntsville, Alabama, and Thome the son of a wealthy slaveholding planter of Augusta, Kentucky. Both came to Lane Seminary, Cincinnati, in 1833, under the influence of Theodore Weld. Both took part in the great debate there, and in the contest over academic freedom, with which we shall deal at length. Both joined the exodus to Oberlin, became antislavery lecturers and ministers, and remained active in the movement until slavery was abolished. Thome went to the British West Indies for the American Anti-Slavery Society in 1836; Allan was undoubtedly the most powerful force in Illinois for freedom after Governor Coles removed to Philadelphia in the early 1830's.

George Bourne was born in Westbury, England, in 1780. He came to America and became pastor of the Presbyterian church at South River, Virginia, in 1814. Two years of contact with slavery so shocked him that he published, in 1816, *The Book and Slavery Irreconcilable*. He was immediately charged with heresy and condemned by the Presbyterian Council. He went to Germantown, Pennsylvania, ultimately joined the Dutch Reformed Church, and wrote some bitter denunciations of slavery: *An Address to the Presbyterian Church, Enforcing the Duty of Excluding All Slaveholders from the "Communion of Saints"; Man Stealing and Slavery Denounced by the Presbyterian and Methodist Churches; Picture of Slavery in the United States of America;* and *Slavery Illustrated in Its Effects upon Women and Domestic Society.* Bourne's attack upon slavery was bold. Some would say that it was extreme, but no one knew better than he the relentless fashion in which the slave power was silencing its critics, and he retaliated in kind.

The list of exiles grows long; but there were others: Andrew Bankson of Tennessee who came to Illinois in 1808, became a state senator, and worked actively in the antislavery cause; William Brisbane of South Carolina who freed his slaves, moved to Cincinnati in 1835 and ultimately to Wisconsin, where he was pastor of the Baptist Church in Madison and chief clerk of the state senate; Alexander Campbell of Virginia, who went to Kentucky in 1796 and to Ripley, Ohio, in 1803, where he freed his slaves, served in the Ohio legislature and in the United States Senate, and became the first vice-president of the Ohio Anti-Slavery Society in 1835; Peter Cartwright, of Virginia, who moved to Kentucky in 1790, and from fear that his daughters would marry slaveholders, to Illinois in 1824, where he served in the state legislature and ran against Lincoln for Congress in 1846; Obed Denham of Virginia, who went to Ohio in 1797, founded the town of Bethel, and endowed a Baptist church for those "who do not hold slaves, nor commune at the Lord's Table with those that do practice such tyranny over their fellow creatures."

Others were William Dunlop who went from Kentucky to Ohio in 1796, freed his slaves and settled them on land near Ripley, and further proved his steadfastness in the cause by paying $1600 for the release of John B. Mahan when he was kidnapped and taken to Kentucky for trial on a charge of abducting slaves; Samuel Grist of Virginia, who bought land in Brown County, Ohio, for one thousand slaves to whom he gave not only farms but livestock and tools; and Risdom Moore, who lived from 1760 until 1812 in his native state of Delaware, then in North Carolina, and then in Georgia, moved to Illinois in the latter year, freed his slaves, served as speaker in the territorial legislature, and as a member of the state legislature, was burned in effigy by proslavery men because of his activities in behalf of the Negroes and against slavery.

This does not by any means exhaust the list. There were hundreds who came North to escape slavery and worked quietly for emancipation in local anti-slavery societies and at the ballot box. There were the two—James G. Birney and Angelina Grimké—whose lives are woven inextricably into every phase of the struggle. Finally, there were the thousands of fugitives who settled in Northern communities and by their industry and good citizenship bore mute testimony of the falsity of the proslavery doctrines, and thousands, too, who bore the indestructible marks of cruelty.

The people who have been here mentioned, with very few exceptions left the South about 1800, shortly before or shortly after the turn of the century, when the Revolutionary impulse for emancipation was checked and the South was dedicated to perpetual slavery. They left because so-called security regulations impinged upon their freedom to discuss slavery, to educate or preach to the slaves, and to ease their distress and set them free; or because they feared the baneful influence of slavery upon their children, or because they lost faith in the future of the slave country. Almost all of them were slaveholders who freed their slaves at tremendous financial sacrifice. There was no quibbling on their part about gradual emancipation, or compensated emancipation, and they did not participate in that refined form of brigandage known as "allowing the slaves to purchase their freedom." They emancipated them, and in most cases brought them North and gave them a start as free men.

These people, also, were not lowly people seeking to improve their economic status. All of them were men of assured positions and security in their communities. If there is one thing crystal clear about the antislavery movement up to this point—and it continued to be true to the end—it is this: *it was an intellectual and moral crusade for social reform and common decency in human relationships, initiated and carried through at great personal sacrifice by men of property and high position in religious and educational institutions, in public life, and in the professions.* These exiles from the South were that kind of people. Those who became active in the agitation against slavery were devoted to the cause and effective in their contributions. One does not ask, *Could slavery have been abolished* without Rankin, Coles, Birney, and Angelina Grimké? One shudders at the possible consequences to the Presbyterian church, to the state of Illinois, to the Constitution, to women's rights, had these great intellects and courageous souls become hostages to the slave power.

JOHN L. THOMAS (1926–   ), associate professor
of American history at Brown University, takes
exception to the views expressed by Rhodes, Barnes,
and Dumond. At first consideration Thomas seems
to provide a synthesis combining elements from both
western revival and traditional New England
interpretations, as he emphasizes the importance
of abolitionism in both areas and asserts that
evangelical ideas provided the ideological basis
for both western and Garrisonian abolitionism.
The crucial point in Thomas' interpretation, however,
is his observation that a majority of western
abolitionists were "transplanted New Englanders."
According to him, earlier interpretations overemphasize
the importance of personalities and geographical
considerations; Rhodes fails to understand,
while Barnes and Dumond deny, that abolitionism
was in fact a product and extension of New England
culture.*

► *Abolitionism: A Product and Extension of New England Culture*

To the young provincial from New-
buryport [William Lloyd Garrison], Boston seemed vast and forbidding in the
cold gray light of December, 1826. . . .

Formidable as it may have appeared
to him, Boston in 1826 was a small city
of some fifty thousand people which still
wore its colonial heritage with pride.
Mayor Josiah Quincy with the blessing
of Boston's first families was just beginning to modernize the city, paving the
streets, building a new city market, and
providing police and fire protection.
Lloyd Garrison caught the unmistakable
air of paternalism blowing down from
Beacon Hill, where merchant families
preserved their conservative opinions as

carefully as their fortunes. . . .

That wealth and position carried responsibilities towards their less fortunate
townsmen, the leading families of Boston
never doubted. Most of the city's social
services were furnished by private charity. Many a Sunday afternoon Garrison
strolled through the common to the
strains of a brass band hired by the
Society for the Suppression of Vice in the
vain hope of emptying the grog shops.
Wives and daughters of the leading citizens devoted leisure hours to such benevolent societies as the Boston Fatherless
and Widow's Society and the Penitent
Female Refuge. By the time Lloyd Garrison arrived charitable associations had

* From *The Liberator: A Biography of William Lloyd Garrison* by John L. Thomas, by permission of Little, Brown, and Co. Copyright © 1963 by John L. Thomas. Pp. 54–73, 163–167.

become a habit with Boston's well-to-do: between 1810 and 1840 they averaged at least one new benevolent institution a year, most of them founded for the dual purpose of attending to the needy and repairing public morals. The logic of Boston paternalism posited social control as well as Christian charity, and the art of using their wealth wisely was one which these families had fully mastered.

If was not to the Boston of Beacon Hill or to the fashionable West End that Garrison went on his arrival, but to the Scott Street boardinghouse of his friend Thomas Bennett, himself a newcomer from the 'Port. Bennett's boardinghouse lay in the heart of another and different society of the middle classes. This was the Boston Emerson meant when he spoke of the city as a moving principle, "a living mind, agitating the mass and always afflicting the conservative class with some odious novelty or other." Middle-class Boston consisted of professional people, small merchants, artisans, and shopkeepers, many of them, like Garrison, recent arrivals from Essex North and the Old Colony. They brought with them a seaboard conservatism and social aspirations which they shared with the patricians, but they wore their conservatism with a difference. In the first place, they disliked the proprietary manner of the old families and resented their institutionalized snobbery. Coming from country strongholds of orthodoxy, they mistrusted the "icy system" of the Unitarianism with its cool lucidities that replaced the majesty of God with the tricks of human reason. The benevolence of Boston merchants stemmed from a recognition of their declining political power, while the religious impulse of middle-class Boston sprang from the rocky soil of Christian zeal.

Garrison's orthodox friends in his adopted city assumed that only Christianity could save the nation from infidelity and licentiousness. They viewed the renovation of American morals as a crusade which could never be won by local contingents of philanthropists dispensing charity and advice but demanded a revolutionary army organized into missionary, tract, and Bible societies captained by the great religious leaders of the day. One of these leaders was their own Lyman Beecher, recently made pastor of the Hanover Street Church. If the spiritual center of Unitarian Boston was Channing's Federal Street congregation, evangelical Boston made its headquarters in the home of Lyman Beecher in the North End next to the old burying ground on Copp's Hill, whither he was known frequently to retire to pray for those whose feet stumbled on the dark mountain. Hanover Street Church became Garrison's spiritual home and Beecher his mentor.

Beecher had also come to Boston in 1826 in response to a challenge. As an organizer and what another age would call a public-relations expert he had few peers. Earlier he had organized the Connecticut Society for the Reformation of Morals to protect the Standing Order against "Sabbath-breakers, rum-sellers, tippling folk, infidels, and ruff scuff" who made up the ranks of democracy. He wrote tracts, held revivals, established a magazine, lectured on temperance, lobbied for Sunday blue laws, and fought manfully to preserve the establishment at every turn. When he finally lost the battle against disestablishment in Connecticut in 1817, he admitted that "it was as dark a day as ever I saw." Presently, however, he saw the light: far from destroying Christian order, disestablishment had actually strengthened it by cutting the churches loose from state support. With missions, revivals, and voluntary associations Christians could exert a far stronger influence than ever they could with shoe buckles, cocked hats, and gold-headed canes. To prove his point Beecher threw himself into the work of Christian reform, fashioning Bible and tract societies, supporting home missions, the temperance cause and all other benevolent associations which sprang up in the East after 1812. Under his aegis these vast interdenominational societies formed a benevolent empire run by an interlocking directorate of lay and clerical figures whose avowed aim was the engineering of mass American consent to Christian leadership.

As the democratization of American church polity proceeded apace, the need for a major theological reorientation grew urgent. This need Beecher and his old Yale classmate, Nathaniel Taylor, attempted to meet with a doctrine of their own. "Beecherism" or "Taylorism" as it was more commonly called, took for its central theme the primacy of reason over the letter of revelation. Men are punished for their sins, Beecher and Taylor argued, only because they freely and willingly choose to sin. Without free agency there could be no sinful act; men are truly free agents. Saving grace lies within the reach of any man who will but try to come to Christ. Sin is selfishness, and regeneration simply the act of will which consists of the preference of God to every other object, that act being the effect of the Holy Spirit operating on the mind. "Whosoever will may come"—this was the real import of their new doctrine which furnished the rationale for the revivals and the benevolent crusade of the Second Great Awakening. In Beecher's new formula piety and ethics, severed in the First

Great Awakening, were reunited in a democratic evangelical puritanism. . . .

To Garrison, who went regularly to hear him preach, there seemed something majestic in this stocky figure with his untidy robes flying behind him as he strode to the pulpit to do battle for the Lord. Beecher was a dynamo. Both the muscularity of his sermons and his devotion to the strenuous life revealed a man of prodigious energy, impatient of all restraint and aching to get on with the business of Christianizing the country. His conversation abounded in military figures—plans of battle, shot and shell, victorious charges, and routing the enemy. Beecher had the kind of Christian belligerence which young Garrison understood. "As a divine," he noted enthusiastically, "Lyman Beecher has no equal." What was it that gave Beecher strength? "Truth—TRUTH—delivered in a child-like simplicity and affection." Sitting in the back pews of the Hanover Street Church, Garrison did not realize yet the full import of Beecher's message or the lengths to which it would carry him. He only knew that Beecher offered revealed religion as a guide; but for a young man intent on directing the lives of other people that was enough. . . .

The editorial opportunity he sought came in the person of the Reverend William Collier, who ran a boardinghouse on Milk Street. Collier was a Baptist city missionary and the editor of a struggling temperance newspaper, the *National Philanthropist*. His boardinghouse served as a haven for missionaries, visiting clergymen, itinerant evangelists and Christian reformers of all kinds; his paper exposed the evils of drink and denounced gambling, prostitution, dueling and theatergoing, and extolled the virtues of Bible societies, home missions, and Sabbath observance. In its pages each week could be found the evangelical prescription for a better world.

At Collier's Garrison met the printer of the *National Philanthropist,* Nathaniel White, who hired him as a typesetter sometime late in 1827. When Collier, discouraged by the anemic circulation of his paper, decided to sell out to his printer, White made Garrison his new editor. On January 4, 1828, the *National Philanthropist* appeared for the first time under new editorial direction, although Garrison's name did not appear on the masthead until March.

. . . In an editorial entitled "Moral Character of Public Men" he expounded his new philosophy of reform. "Moral principles should be inseparably connected with political; and the splendid talents of the dissolute must not be preferred to the competent, though inferior, abilities of the virtuous of our land." Americans, he continued, had never understood the need for a moral influence sufficient to control party intemperance and enhance the value of public opinion. It therefore behooved Christians especially to guard against "the common partialities of political strife." Political parties should henceforth be subject to Christian control. No longer would the duelist, the gambler, the debaucher, or the "profane swearer" be elected simply because he was a Federalist or a Republican. Political morality must be raised to the level of Christian behavior. "It is due to our principles, our civil, social and moral institutions, that men whose characters are notoriously bad should be deprived of the control of our political destinies."

There was nothing new in Garrison's plea for religious influence in politics; it had been the stock-in-trade of evangelicals and their benevolent societies for fifteen years. Behind its seemingly non-partisan appeal lay the conservative opinions of clericals who sought to defend the established order from onrushing democracy. One of the most striking of the many ironies that studded Garrison's career was the fact that his antislavery radicalism evolved out of a literal interpretation of these principles of Christian conservatism.

The professed aim of the benevolent societies which sprang up after 1812 in response to the challenge of democracy was the extension of the Christian faith and the reformation of public morals. The American Bible Society, the Sunday School Union, the American Tract Society, home and foreign missionary societies all shared the common goal of educating the citizen for participation in a Christian America. The publications of the Bible Society urged its members to scrutinize voting lists and elect only Christian candidates. The Society for the preservation of the Sabbath discredited any office-seeker who failed to keep the Sabbath. The Temperance Society withheld its support from any politician known to imbibe. And so it went. Denied entrance to the halls of state through the main portals, the ministers availed themselves of the back door. If they could not make the laws themselves, they could see to it that the laws recognized their influence. By the time Garrison joined them, the benevolent societies were busy as never before operating a gigantic political lobby, publicity bureau, and propaganda machine in the interests of the new puritanism.

When it came to defining the Christian statesman the evangelical formula grew blurred. It was all well and good to insist on honesty, trust, duty, and uprightness, but what did these words really mean? Granted that the unregenerate politician could be identified by his sins —tippling, gambling, and general licentious behavior, but the positive content of the ideal of Christian statesmanship remained unexplored. The evangelical argument ran like this: A "professing Christian" is one who is regenerate (i.e., has received saving grace) and is thus free from selfishness, hypocrisy and dishonesty. Once in office he is bound to make the right decisions. His views on the tariff, land grants, or the Bank hardly matter since he can *always* be trusted to reach a Christian solution. On the theory that it takes a Christian to recognize and elect a fellow communicant, the evangelicals argued that social reform really begins with the moral reform of individuals. Not until everyone is purified can the problem of Christian government be solved. Poverty, slavery, capital punishment, imprisonment for debt, extension of the franchise, all the major social problems await the regeneration of the individual. Once the saints are legion they will make their righteousness felt, and their moral omnicompetence will ensure a reign of peace and justice.

Thus the problems of social and political reform were reduced in the evangelical equation to elements of personal morality. By reforming the individual and bringing him to Christ the preacher would mysteriously change his heart and thereby qualify him for leadership. Piecemeal reforms, especially those favored by political parties and disaffected minorities, they dismissed as pernicious half-measures based on compromise rather than the rock of universal love.

Such in all its essentials was the doctrine of moral reform as Garrison understood and accepted it, an equation of duties and rewards. "If we have hitherto lived without reference to another state of existence," he wrote in one of his new editorials, "let us do so no longer." The fruits of earth are bitter. Christians must lay up treasures in heaven "where change and decay have never entered, and the ardent aspirations of the soul are satisfied in the fulness of God." The balm of Gilead alone can restore peace to the troubled, health to the wounded, and happiness to the suffering: "its application will make men the heirs of joyous immortality; and thanks to the great Physician of souls, this sovereign balm can be obtained without money and without price." Faith without works, however, was not enough. The very certainty of Christian truth dictated the need for an immediate reform of the evils of the world....

From now on, he promised, his methods would be those of Christian example and enterprise. "The gospel of Christ breathes peace to men," he explained, "its language is full of the mildness of God.... This gospel is not to be propagated by fire and sword, nor nourished by blood and slaughter. It must go forth under the banner of the cross." Beneath that banner in the years to come he would collect a band of militant Christian rebels who cared less for the mildness of God than for their freedom of conscience....

Though he scarcely realized it, his belief in moral progress harmonized completely with the confident outlook of the Jacksonian age. In 1828 Senator Richard M. Johnson, spokesman for the New West and archenemy of the New England clergy, delivered an oration on the Senate floor in which he prophesied unlimited progress as the American destiny. Reading Johnson's speech, Garrison was moved to add an editorial comment of his own. . . . America's future, he concluded, was unlimited, with population expanding, a government based on equality of rights, humanity and justice blended with religious principle. Why should the Republic crumble or dissolve?

Garrison's hymn to progress formed part of the liturgy of evangelicalism. For all their jeremiads and professional pessimism the American evangelicals were the unwitting carriers of the Revolutionary heritage. Their faith in the efficacy of voluntary associations revealed a deep commitment to the doctrine of progress. They believed that they could convert a wicked nation to goodness simply by organizing and directing public opinion, that is, by the judicious use of Christian pressure groups. But who could say where this process might end? In stressing the importance of public opinion they gave their own meaning to the ideal of democratic association, but their vision of progress and their ideal of the free individual were fundamentally similar to the perfectionist image of the Jeffersonians. True, they cried down natural reason and the Enlightenment world view. Nevertheless, their acceptance of the principle of free association and their certainty of the power of revealed truth to win in the open market sustained and carried forward the optimism of the Revolutionary generation. In perfecting their scheme for a stable society strong in religious habit and united in the Protestant faith they discovered the very democratic techniques which were soon to be turned against them. The whole benevolent apparatus—open societies, public meetings, free literature, propaganda—which they used to impose a conservative Christian pattern on American

society might as easily be appropriated by another group of reformers with a more explosive cause. Tracts, newspapers and placards, so effective in fighting Sabbath-breaking and the Sunday mails, could also be used to free the slaves. In the principle of voluntary association they had found an effective method for agitating causes which could divide as well as unify the country. Had they but known it, the evangelicals had fashioned an engine of national self-destruction. All that logic required was a man who practiced the Christian zeal they preached.

Gradually Garrison began to distinguish between complaints of irreligious behavior and major social evils. He continued to lash out at profane language and licentiousness, at habits like "the present rage of sporting huge mustaches," but he was slowly discovering that there were certain questions to which the evangelicals had no easy answers. One of these was William Ladd's peace question and the problem of defensive war. Indifference to principle nettled him. If war was morally wrong, how could defensive war be right? If slavery was un-Christian, why did Christians practice it? What could be more reasonable than the attempt to live by the all-sufficent word of God? The more he pondered the gospel of Christ the closer he was drawn to its simple message—"Go ye and do likewise." The theological implications of Christian perfectionism were not yet clear to him. Just how truth could be gleaned from the chaff of Biblical contradictions he did not as yet know. He was satisfied to consult his conscience and then act.

In this mood of self-examination he approached the problem of American apathy. What but "indifference" explained the reluctance of Christians to undertake the work of reform? "There are, in faith, few *reasoning* Christians," he wrote; "the majority of them are swayed more by the usages of the world than by any definite perception of what constitutes duty." Was there not enough Christian influence in the country to reform it?

By the "duty of reasoning Christians" he did not mean simply the common-sense adaptations of religious precepts to daily life, but a purer and more personal belief in the superiority of the righteous man. Slavery and war, vices "incorporated into the existence of society," could only be corrected by re-fashioning America according to the word of God. The errors of the evangelicals, he saw, lay not in their ideals but in their failure to live up to them. It was a question of fundamentals—spiritual principles were levers for moving the world, social action a form of personal atonement. Slowly he was learning that evangelical passion logically ends in radicalism; further, that perfectionism and radicalism are similar states of mind. In the consistency with which he pursued his discovery lay the profound unity of his life. . . .

One of the myths that attach themselves to the American radical is that of rugged independence. The image of the lone figure struggling against overwhelming odds is a naturally appealing one to an age that enjoys chiefly the nostalgia of the history of American radicalism. Garrison was the willing perpetrator of just such a myth. He liked to tell how, unaided and alone, he found his way to abolition and formed the crusade that eventually freed the Negro. This legend, carefully nurtured by his followers, ensured his fame but obscured

the debts he owed to others. Beecher and Boston supplied him with most of the causes and techniques he used in the anti-slavery cause. Long after he denounced Beecher and the evangelicals he remained obligated to them for the convictions which led him to racial equality. He came to Boston a brash young man without a cause; he left eighteen months later sure that he had found one. The year 1828 was his *annus mirabilis* for which the evangelicals had prepared him. . . .

American abolitionism from its inception was the product of two distinct groups, one in New England under Garrison, the other in New York and the Ohio Valley under transplanted New Englanders like Theodore Weld, Beriah Green, Elizur Wright and Henry Stanton. As a patron of American reform with connections in both the East and West, Arthur Tappan was a pivotal figure in the formation of a national anti-slavery society. His New York Committee served as a clearinghouse for abolitionist projects, distributed information, and functioned as a directory for reformers everywhere. It was Tappan's great achievement in the year 1833 to join together the Eastern and Western branches of the anti-slavery movement into a single national organ, an achievement which no amount of Garrisonian disparagement could ever undo.

Tappan's interest in the West dated from the autumn of 1829 and the appearance in New York City of the great revivalist Charles Grandison Finney. If Lyman Beecher served as the archpriest of the eastern half of the Benevolent Empire, the New West belonged to Finney. Just as Beecher's version of "immediate repentence" provided the theo-

logical underpinnings for Garrisonism, so
Finney's Arminian doctrine of the "new
heart," at once simpler and bolder than
Beecher's, supplied the rationale for
Western anti-slavery.

Tappan's lieutenant and the leader of
the Western anti-slavery movement was
a convert of Finney's, Theodore Weld,
an unkempt, sad-eyed evangelical whose
quiet intensity and natural shrewdness
brought him quickly to the front of
the movement. Modest and circumspect
as he seemed, Weld was a natural leader
of men, an astute judge of character,
and an efficient organizer—all the things
that Garrison was not. He had been lec-
turing on the temperance circuit when
the Tappans, struck by his promotional
talent and forceful presence, decided to
have the sole use of so brilliant a lecturer
and gave him the job of raising funds
and selecting the site for a great theological seminary in the West based on
the manual labor plan. In the fall of
1831, while Garrison was busy sending
copies of the *Liberator* into the Ohio
Valley, Weld set out on a tour of the
West and South, addressing legislatures,
colleges, churches and philanthropists
on the subject of manual labor. His campaign took him as far south as Huntsville, Alabama, where he met James G.
Birney, an earnest young country lawyer
whose austere Presbyterian conscience
had convinced him of the wrongfulness
of slavery. Just as Garrison had first
turned hopefully to the American Colonization Society for an answer to the
problem, so Birney and Weld studied the
society's program and weighed the justice
of returning the Negro to Africa.
Though Weld could not doubt the sinfulness of slavery, as yet he knew little
about it, and Birney's searching questions and Scriptural arguments set him

thinking. His effect on the Alabama
lawyer was no less pronounced: when
Weld started north after nearly a month
in Huntsville, Birney abandoned a flour-
ishing legal practice to become an agent
of the American Colonization Society.

From now on Weld, like Garrison before him, occupied himself almost exclusively with the study of American
slavery. The turning point in his career
came with his visit to the wilderness
campus of Western Reserve College in
Hudson, Ohio, late in November 1832.
Here he met Elizur Wright and Beriah
Green, two faculty members who had
been converted to abolition by Garrison's
Thoughts. . . . "You will recollect,"
Wright admitted to Garrison soon after
his talks with Weld, "that in a letter
some time ago, I expressed some doubts
with regard to the correctness of your
views in respect to the African colony.
Your 'Thoughts on African Colonization' have dispelled these doubts. I find
that I was misinformed, as doubtless
thousands are, in regard to your opinions." Using Garrison's moral arguments,
Wright and Green converted Weld to
immediate emancipation and convinced
him that "the very first business is to
shove off the lubberly Colonization
Society which is, at the very best, a super-
imposed dead weight." Such was Garrison's message as the faculty at Western
Reserve interpreted it. "The question
now is, what shall be done?" Wright
wrote to Weld in December. "We would
put one hundred copies of the *Liberator*
into as many towns on the Reserve, if
we knew where to find the means." They
planned to form a local anti-slavery
society, he told Weld, but what was
needed was a national organization along
the lines of the other benevolent societies. "What would benevolent men in

New York think of a convention on this subject, about the time of the anniversaries next spring?"

As he traveled east to New York City in January, 1833, Weld was pondering Wright's suggestion when he received a letter from Garrison inviting him to Boston to address the New England Society on the subject of manual labor. Weld refused, pleading prior engagements in New York City. "Besides, Sir," he went on, "I am ignorant of the history, specific plans, modes of operation, present position and ultimate aims of the N. E. Anti-Slavery Society. Residing in the interior of the state of New York, I have been quite out of range of its publications, have never seen any of them or indeed *any* expose of its operations, and all the definite knowledge of its plans and principles which I possess has been thro the perversions and distortions of its avowed opposers." Yet he could see by the *"expressive name"* of Garrison's organization that its sentiments agreed with his—that

Nothing but crime can forfeit liberty. That no condition of birth, no shade of color, no mere misfortune of circumstance, can annul that birth-right charter, which God has bequeathed to every being upon whom he has stamped his own image, by making him a *free moral agent,* and that he who robs his fellow-man of this tramples upon right, subverts justice, outrages humanity, unsettles the foundations of human safety and sacrilegiously assumes the prerogatives of God; and further, that he who retains by force, and refuses to surrender that which was originally obtained by violence or fraud, is joint partner in the original sin, becomes its apologist and makes it the business of every moment to perpetuate it afresh, however he may lull his conscience by the vain pleas of expediency or necessity.

Reading Weld's letter, the very phrases of which were familiar, Garrison recognized his own arguments from the pen of a man who had never even heard of him. The *Liberator* had done its work well on the Western Reserve.

In contrast to Barnes, Dumond, and Thomas, DAVID DONALD (1920–   ), professor of American history at The Johns Hopkins University, views evangelical revivalism as a surface manifestation of abolitionist fervor rather than a fundamental reason for its emergence during the 1830s. According to him, abolitionist leadership was provided by a displaced social elite, the sons and daughters of old and socially prominent New England families whose traditional leadership in political and economic affairs had been pre-empted by a rising class of industrialists, merchant princes, and corporation lawyers. Abolitionism was not only a crusade to free the slave, but an attempt by antislavery radicals to reassert "the traditional values of their class at home."*

Abolitionist Leadership: A Displaced Social Elite

The abolitionist . . . was a special type of antislavery agitator, and his crusade was part of that remarkable American social phenomenon which erupted in the 1830's, "freedom's ferment," the effervescence of kindred humanitarian reform movements—prohibition; prison reform, education for the blind, deaf, dumb; world peace; penny postage; women's rights; and a score of lesser and more eccentric drives.

Historians have been so absorbed in chronicling what these movements did, in allocating praise or blame among squabbling factions in each, and in making moral judgments on the desirability of various reforms that they have paid surprisingly little attention to the move-ment as a whole. Few serious attempts have been made to explain why humanitarian reform appeared in America when it did, and more specifically why immediate abolitionism, so different in tone, method, and membership from its predecessors and its successor, emerged in the 1830's.

The participants in such movements naturally give no adequate explanation for such a causal problem. According to their voluminous memoirs and autobiographies, they were simply convinced by religion, by reading, by reflection that slavery was evil, and they pledged their lives and their sacred honor to destroy it. Seeing slavery in a Southern state, reading an editional by William Lloyd Garri-

* Reprinted from *Lincoln Reconsidered* by David Donald, by permission of Alfred A. Knopf, Inc. Copyright © 1956 by David Donald. Pp. 21–36.

son, hearing a sermon by Theodore Dwight Weld—such events precipitated a decision made on the highest of moral and ethical planes. No one who has studied the abolitionist literature can doubt the absolute sincerity of these accounts. Abolitionism was a dangerous creed of devotion, and no fair-minded person can believe that men joined the movement for personal gain or for conscious self-glorification. In all truth, the decision to become an antislavery crusader was a decision of conscience.

But when all this is admitted, there are still fundamental problems. Social evils are always present; vice is always in the saddle while virtue trudges on afoot. Not merely the existence of evil but the recognition of it is the prerequisite for reform. Were there more men of integrity, were there more women of sensitive conscience in the 1830's than in any previous decade? A generation of giants these reformers were indeed, but why was there such a concentration of genius in those ten years from 1830 to 1840? If the individual's decision to join the abolitionist movement was a matter of personality or religion or philosophy, is it not necessary to inquire why so many similar personalities or religions or philosophies appeared in America simultaneously? In short, we need to know why so many Americans in the 1830's were predisposed toward a certain kind of reform movement.

Many students have felt, somewhat vaguely, this need for a social interpretation of reform. Little precise analysis has been attempted, but the general histories of antislavery attribute the abolitionist movement to the Christian tradition, to the spirit of the Declaration of Independance, to the ferment of Jacksonian democracy, or to the growth of romanticism. That some or all of these factors

may have relation to abolitionism can be granted, but this helps little. Why did the "spirit of Puritanism," to which one writer attributes the movement, become manifest as militant abolitionism in the 1830's although it had no such effect on the previous generation? Why did the Declaration of Independence find fulfillment in abolition during the sixth decade after its promulgation, and not in the fourth or the third?

In their elaborate studies of the antislavery movement, Gilbert H. Barnes and Dwight L. Dumond have pointed up some of the more immediate reasons for the rise of American abolitionism. Many of the most important antislavery leaders fell under the influence of Charles Grandison Finney, whose revivalism set rural New York and the Western Reserve ablaze with religious fervor and evoked "Wonderful outpourings of the Holy Spirit" throughout the North. Not merely did Finney's invocation of the fear of hell and the promise of heaven rouse sluggish souls to renewed religious zeal, but his emphasis upon good works and pious endeavor as steps toward salvation freed men's minds from the bonds of arid theological controversies. One of Finney's most famous converts was Theodore Dwight Weld, the greatest of the Western abolitionists, "eloquent as an angel and powerful as thunder," who recruited a band of seventy antislavery apostles, trained them in Finney's revivalistic techniques, and sent them forth to consolidate the emancipation movement in the North. Their greatest successes were reaped in precisely those communities where Finney's preaching had prepared the soil.

Barnes and Dumond also recognized the importance of British influence upon the American antislavery movement. The connection is clear and easily traced: British antislavery leaders fought for immediate emancipation in the West Indies; reading the tracts of Wilberforce and Clarkson converted William Lloyd Garrison to immediate abolitionism at about the same time that Theodore Weld was won over to the cause by his English friend Charles Stuart; and Weld in turn gained for the movement the support of the Tappan brothers, the wealthy New York merchants and philanthropists who contributed so much in money and time to the antislavery crusade. Thus, abolition had in British precedent a model, in Garrison and Weld leaders, and in the Tappans financial backers.

Historians are deeply indebted to Professors Barnes and Dumond, for the importance of their studies on the antislavery movement is very great. But perhaps they have raised as many questions as they have answered. Both religious revivalism and British antislavery theories had a selective influence in America. Many men heard Finney and Weld, but only certain communities were converted. Hundreds of Americans read Wilberforce, Clarkson, and the other British abolitionists, but only the Garrisons and the Welds were convinced. The question remains: Whether they received the idea through the revivalism of Finney or through the publications of British antislavery spokesmen, why were some Americans in the 1830's for the first time moved to advocate immediate abolition? Why was this particular seed bed ready at this precise time?

II

I believe that the best way to answer this difficult question is to analyze the leadership of the abolitionist movement. There is, unfortunately, no complete list of American abolitionists, and I have had to use a good deal of subjective judgment in drawing up a roster of leading reformers. From the classified indexes of the *Dictionary of American Biography* and the old Appleton's *Cyclopaedia of American Biography* and from important primary and secondary works on the reform generation, I made a list of about two hundred and fifty persons who seemed to be identified with the antislavery cause. This obviously is not a definitive enumeration of all the important abolitionists; had someone else compiled it, other names doubtless would have been included. Nevertheless, even if one or two major spokesmen have accidentally been omitted, this is a good deal more than a representative sampling of antislavery leadership.

After preliminary work I eliminated nearly one hundred of these names. Some proved not to be genuine abolitionists but advocates of colonizing the freed Negroes in Africa; others had only incidental interest or sympathy for emancipation. I ruthlessly excluded those who joined the abolitionists after 1840, because the political antislavery movement clearly poses a different set of causal problems. After this weeding out, I had reluctantly to drop other names because I was unable to secure more than random bits of information about them. Some of Weld's band of seventy agitators, for instance, were so obscure that even Barnes and Dumond were unable to identify them. There remained the names of one hundred and six abolitionists, the hard core of active antislavery leadership in the 1830's.

Most of these abolitionists were born between 1790 and 1810, and when the first number of the *Liberator* was published in 1831, their median age was twenty-nine. Abolitionism was thus a revolt of the young.

My analysis confirms the traditional identification of radical antislavery with New England. Although I made every effort to include Southern and Western leaders, eighty-five per cent of these abolitionists came from Northeastern states, sixty per cent from New England, thirty per cent from Massachusetts alone. Many of the others were descended from New England families. Only four of the leaders were born abroad or were second-generation immigrants.

The ancestors of these abolitionists are in some ways as interesting as the antislavery leaders themselves. In the biographies of their more famous descendants certain standard phrases recur: "of the best New England stock," of "Pilgrim descent," "of a serious, pious household." The parents of the leaders generally belonged to a clearly defined stratum of society. Many were preachers, doctors, or teachers; some were farmers and a few were merchants; but only three were manufacturers (and two of these on a very small scale), none was a banker, and only one was an ordinary day laborer. Virtually all the parents were staunch Federalists.

These families were neither rich nor poor, and it is worth remembering that among neither extreme did abolitionism flourish. The abolitionist could best appeal to "the substantial men" of the community, thought Weld, and not to "the *aristocracy* and fashionable worldliness" that remained aloof from reform. In *The Burned-Over District,* an important analysis of reform drives in western New York, Whitney R. Cross has confirmed Weld's social analysis. In New York, antislavery was strongest in those counties which had once been economically dominant but which by the 1830's though still prosperous, had relatively fallen behind their more advantageously situated neighbors. As young men the fathers of abolitionists had been leaders of their communities and states; in their old age they were elbowed aside by the merchant prince, the manufacturing tycoon, the corporation lawyer. The bustling democracy of the 1830's passed them by; as the Reverend Ludovicus Weld lamented to his famous son Theodore: "I have . . . felt like a stranger in a strange land."

If the abolitionists were descendants of old and distinguished New England families, it is scarcely surprising to find among them an enthusiasm for higher education. The women in the movement could not, of course, have much formal education, nor could the three Negroes here included, but of the eighty-nine white male leaders, at least fifty-three attended college, university, or theological seminary. In the East, Harvard and Yale were the favored schools; in the West, Oberlin; but in any case the training was usually of the traditional liberal-arts variety.

For an age of chivalry and repression there was an extraordinary proportion of women in the abolitionist movement. Fourteen of these leaders were women who defied the convention that the female's place was at the fireside, not in the forum, and appeared publicly as antislavery apostles. The Grimké sisters of South Carolina were the most famous of these, but most of the antislavery heroines came from New England.

It is difficult to tabulate the religious affiliations of antislavery leaders. Most were troubled by spiritual discontent, and they wandered from one sect to another seeking salvation. It is quite clear, however, that there was a heavy Congregational-Presbyterian and Quaker preponderance. There were many Methodists, some Baptists, but very few Unitarians, Episcopalians, or Catholics. Recent admirable dissertations on the antislavery movement in each of the Western states, prepared at the University of Michigan under Professor Dumond's supervision, confirm the conclusion that, except in Pennsylvania, it is correct to consider humanitarian reform and Congregational-Presbyterianism as causally interrelated.

Only one of these abolitionist leaders seems to have had much connection with the rising industrialism of the 1830's, and only thirteen of the entire group were born in any of the principal cities of the United States. Abolition was distinctly a rural movement, and throughout the crusade many of the antislavery leaders seemed to feel an instinctive antipathy toward the city. Weld urged his following: "Let the great cities *alone;* they must be burned down by *back fires.* The springs to touch in order to move them *lie in the country."*

In general the abolitionists had little sympathy or understanding for the problems of an urban society. Reformers though they were, they were men of conservative economic views. Living in an age of growing industrialization, of tenement congestion, of sweatshop oppression, not one of them can properly be identified with the labor movement of the 1830's. Most would agree with Garrison, who denounced labor leaders for trying "to inflame the minds of our working classes against the more opulent, and to persuade men that they are contemned and oppressed by a wealthy aristocracy." After all, Wendell Phillips assured the laborers, the American factory operative could be "neither wronged nor oppressed" so long as he had the ballot. William Ellery Channing, gentle high priest of the Boston area, told dissatisfied miners that moral self-improvement was a more potent weapon than strikes, and he urged that they take advantage of the leisure afforded by unemployment for mental and spiritual self-cultivation. A Massachusetts attempt to limit the hours of factory operatives to ten a day was denounced by Samuel Gridley Howe, veteran of a score of humanitarian wars, as "emasculating the people" because it took from them their free right to choose their conditions of employment.

The suffering of laborers during periodic depressions aroused little sympathy among abolitionists. As Emerson remarked tartly, "Do not tell me . . . of my obligation to put all poor men in good situations. Are they *my* poor? I tell thee, thou foolish philanthropist, that I grudge the dollar, the dime, the cent I give to such men. . . ."

Actually it is clear that abolitionists were not so much hostile to labor as indifferent to it. The factory worker represented an alien and unfamiliar system toward which the antislavery leaders felt no kinship or responsibility. Sons of the old New England of Federalism, farming, and foreign commerce, the reformers did not fit into the society that was beginning to be dominated by a bourgeoisie based on manufacturing and trade. Thoreau's bitter comment, "We do not ride on the railroads; they ride on us," was more than the acid aside of a man whose privacy at Walden had been invaded; it was the reaction of a class whose leadership had been discarded. The bitterest attacks in the journals of Ralph Waldo Emerson, the most pointed denunciations in the sermons of Theodore Parker, the harshest philippics in the orations of Charles Sumner were directed against the "Lords of the Loom," not so much for exploiting their labor as for changing the character and undermining the morality of Old New England.

As Lewis Tappan pointed out in a pamphlet suggestively titled *Is It Right to Be Rich?*, reformers did not object to ordinary acquisition of money. It was instead that "eagerness to amass property" which made a man "selfish, unsocial, mean, tyrannical, and but a nominal Christian" that seemed so wrong. It is worth noting that Tappan, in his numerous examples of the vice of excessive accumulation, found this evil stemming from manufacturing and banking, and never from farming or foreign trade —in which last occupation Tappan himself flourished.

Tappan, like Emerson, was trying to uphold the old standards and to protest against the easy morality of the new age. "The invasion of Nature by Trade with its Money, its Credit, its Steam, its Railroads," complained Emerson, "threatens to upset the balance of man, and establish a new universal monarchy more tyrannical than Babylon or Rome." Calmly Emerson welcomed the panic of 1837 as a wholesome lesson to the new monarchs of manufacturing: "I see good in such emphatic and universal calamity. . . ."

Jacksonian democracy, whether considered a labor movement or a triumph of laissez-faire capitalism, obviously had little appeal for the abolitionist conservative. As far as can be determined, only one of these abolitionist leaders was a Jacksonian; nearly all were strong Whigs. William Lloyd Garrison made his first public apperance in Boston to endorse the arch-Whig Harrison Gray Otis; James G. Birney campaigned throughout Alabama to defeat Jackson; Henry B. Stanton wrote editorials for anti-Jackson newspapers. Not merely the leaders but their followers as well seem to have been hostile to Jacksonian democracy, for it is estimated that fifty-nine out of sixty Massachusetts abolitionists belonged to the Whig party.

Jacksonian Democrats recognized the opposition of the abolitionists and accused the leaders of using slavery to distract public attention from more immediate economic problems at home. "The abolitionists of the North have mistaken the color of the American slaves," Theophilus Fisk wrote tartly; "all the real Slaves in the United States have pale faces. . . . I will venture to affirm that there are more slaves in Lowell and Nashua alone than can be found South of the Potomac."

III

Here, then, is a composite portrait of abolitionist leadership. Descended from old and socially dominant Northeastern families, reared in a faith of aggressive piety and moral endeavor, educated for conservative leadership, those young men and women who reached maturity in the 1830's faced a strange and hostile world. Social and economic leadership was being transferred from the country to the city, from the farmer to the manufacturer, from the preacher to the corporation attorney. Too distinguished a family, too gentle an education, too nice a morality were handicaps in a bustling world of business. Expecting to lead, these young people found no followers. They were an elite without function, a displaced class in American society.

Some—like Daniel Webster—made their terms with the new order and lent their talents and their family names to the greater glorification of the god of trade. But many of the young men were unable to overcome their traditional disdain for the new money-grubbing class that was beginning to rule. In these plebeian days they could not be successful in politics; family tradition and education prohibited idleness; and agitation allowed the only chance for personal and social self-fulfillment.

If the young men were aliens in the new industrial society, the young women felt equally lost. Their mothers had married preachers, doctors, teachers, and had become dominant moral forces in their communities. But in rural New England of the 1830's the westward exodus had thinned the ranks of eligible suitors, and because girls of distinguished family hesitated to work in the cotton mills, more and more turned to school-teaching and nursing and other socially useful but unrewarding spinster tasks. The women, like the men, were ripe for reform.

They did not support radical economic reforms because fundamentally these young men and women had no serious quarrel with the capitalistic system of private ownership and control of property. What they did question, and what they did rue, was the transfer of leadership to the wrong groups in society, and their appeal for reform was a strident call for their own class to re-exert its former social dominance. Some fought for prison reform; some for women's rights; some for world peace; but ultimately most came to make that natural identification between moneyed aristocracy, textile-manufacturing, and Southern slave-grown cotton. An attack on slavery was their best, if quite unconscious, attack upon the new industrial system. As Richard Henry Dana, Jr., avowed: "I am a Free Soiler, because I am . . . of the stock of the old Northern gentry, and have a particular dislike to any subserviency

on the part of our people to the slave-holding oligarchy"—and, he might have added, to their Northern manufacturing allies.

With all its dangers and all its sacrifices, membership in a movement like abolitionism offered these young people a chance for a reassertion of their traditional values, an opportunity for association with others of their kind, and a possibility of achieving that self-fulfillment which should traditionally have been theirs as social leaders. Reform gave meaning to the lives of this displaced social elite. "My life, what has it been?" queried one young seeker, "the panting of a soul after eternity—the feeling that there was nothing here to fill the aching void, to provide enjoyment and occupation such as my spirit panted for. The world, what has it been? a howling wilderness. I seem to be just now awakened . . . to a true perception of the end of my being, my duties, my responsibilities, the rich and perpetual pleasures which God has provided for us the fulfillment of duty to Him and to our fellow creatures. Thanks to the A[nti]. S[lavery]. cause, it first gave an impetus to my palsied intellect. . . ."

Viewed against the backgrounds and common ideas of its leaders, abolitionism appears to have been a double crusade. Seeking freedom for the Negro in the South, these reformers wre also attempting a restoration of the traditional values of their class at home. Leadership of humanitarian reform may have been influenced by revivalism or by British precedent, but its true origin lay in the drastic dislocation of Northern society. Basically, abolitionism should be considered the anguished protest of an aggrieved class against a world they never made.

In this selection ROBERT A. SKOTHEIM (1933–   ),
assistant professor of American history at
Wayne State University, challenges the validity
of Donald's "status revolution" thesis. Donald's
interpretation is not only unclear in some ways,
Skotheim maintains, but does not provide the
comparative evidence necessary to substantiate it.*

The "Status Revolution" Thesis Criticized

The concept of a "status revolution" as the basic explanation for abolitionism is a rich one, analogous to Richard Hofstadter's "status revolution" interpretation of the rise of progressivism in the early 1900's.[1] One need not doubt the brilliance of Donald's central idea even though one is compelled to raise certain questions concerning the methods employed in the study and presentation of evidence in the essay itself. These questions relate primarily to one general issue: Is it clear whom in the antislavery movement Donald is describing and at-

tempting to analyze? That is, with whom and in what geographical areas and during which years is Donald concerned? An attempt to answer these questions leads beyond the problem of ascertaining the meaning of the essay to broader problems of historical method.

Although the title is "Toward a Reconsideration of Abolitionists," the essay itself concerns only abolitionist leaders and not the rank and file. The precise relationship which may exist between conclusions relating to abolitionist leadership and conclusions concerning the total number of abolitionists is not expressed. Donald clearly assumes, how-

[1] Richard Hofstadter, *The Age of Reform; from Bryan to F.D.R.* (New York, 1956), Ch. 4.

* From Robert A. Skotheim, "A Note on Historical Method: David Donald's 'Toward a Reconsideration of Abolitionists,' " *Journal of Southern History*, XXV (August, 1959), 356–365. Reprinted with most of the footnotes omitted by permission of the managing editor of the *Journal of Southern History*. Copyright © 1959 by the Southern Historical Association.

ever, that there is an import relationship, for he draws conclusions relating to "abolitionism" on the basis of his conclusions concerning only "abolitionist leaders." Further, the essay discusses how he selected the particular leaders:

There is, unfortunately, no complete list of American abolitionists, and I have had to use a good deal of subjective judgment in drawing up a roster of leading reformers. From the classified indexes of the *Dictionary of American Biography* and the old Appleton's *Cyclopaedia of American Biography* and from important primary and secondary works on the reform generation, I made a list of about two hundred and fifty persons who seemed to be indentified with the antislavery cause. This obviously is not a definitive enumeration of all the important abolitionists; had someone else compiled it, other names doubtless would have been included. Nevertheless, even if one or two major spokesmen have accidentally been omitted, this is a good deal more than a representative sampling of antislavery leadership.

After preliminary work I eliminated nearly one hundred of these names. Some proved not to be genuine abolitionists but advocates of colonizing the freed Negroes in Africa; others had only incidental interest or sympathy for emancipation. I ruthlessly excluded those who joined the abolitionists after 1840, because the political antislavery movement clearly poses a different set of causal problems.

Thus the criterion of abolitionist "leadership" is not officeholding or certain behavior or money contribution, but whether names "seemed to be identified with the antislavery cause" in the literature on the subject, provided that they were "genuine abolitionists" as opposed to individuals who desired colonization for the Negroes in Africa, and provided further that they had become abolitionists before 1840.

The list of names was reduced still

further by inability to obtain information about certain individuals.

After this weeding out [described in the quotation], I had reluctantly to drop other names because I was unable to secure more than random bits of information about them. . . . There remained the names of one hundred and six abolitionists, the hard core of active antislavery leadership in the 1830's.

Donald, after thus describing explicitly the manner in which names of the 106 abolitionist leaders were selected, does not give the names. Nor does he identify them precisely in terms of geographical location or their attitudes toward slavery.

Concerning the geographical background of the 106 leaders, Donald states:

My analysis confirms the traditional identification of radical antislavery with New England. Although I made every effort to include Southern and Western leaders, eighty-five per cent of these abolitionists came from Northeastern states, sixty per cent from New England, thirty per cent from Massachusetts alone. Many of the others were descended from New England families. Only four of the leaders were born abroad or were second-generation immigrants.

In what sense does the essay mean that the "analysis confirms the tradtional identification of radical antislavery with New England?" Does it refute Gilbert Barnes' thesis that the Midwest rather than New England was the home of abolitionism? No answers to these questions are forthcoming, as Donald fails to define "New Englander," though the term apparently means New England birth.... If the names of the 106 abolitionists had been given, one could test Donald's definition as well as ascertain whether his hypothesis is based upon the same individuals studied by Barnes and other students of abolitionists, or whether additional abolitionists are studied. It is impossible to determine these matters from the essay in its present form.

Similarly, the essay does not precisely identify the 106 abolitionists in terms of their attitudes toward slavery. This failure to specify unambiguously the phase of the antislavery movement to which the thesis is meant to apply does not result from a failure to define terms, but rather from the failure to cite examples of abolitionism consistent with the given definitions. Donald clearly says in certain passages that he is not concerned with individuals who became abolitionists after 1840. In the same vein, he explains that he is concerned only with the abolitionism of the 1830's. The demand of the abolitionists

for an unconditional and immediate end of slavery, which first became articulate around 1830, was different from earlier antislavery sentiment, which had focused on gradual emancipation with colonization of the freed Negroes. And the abolitionist movement, with its Garrisonian depreciation of political action, was also distinct from political antislavery, which became dominant in the 1840's.

Thus, the definition of abolitionism in the essay is clear.

It is not clear, however, whether the individuals discussed always fit the terms of the definition. For example, the focus is at times on the abolitionist critics of Lincoln during the Civil War. Donald describes Lincoln's actions in the war and queries why abolitionists were critical of the President. But who are these abolitionists to whom Donald refers? . . . Does Donald mean that the abolitionists of the 1860's were the same people as the abolitionists of the 1830's? Does he mean that he is attempting to explain the behavior of only those abolitionists in the 1860's who had been abolitionists during the 1830's?

The same ambiguity is illustrated by the citing of Richard Henry Dana, Jr., as an example of the dislocated New England antislavery man. . . . Dana's biographer does not describe Dana as an abolitionist in the 1830's, but cites letters in which Dana identifies himself as a Free Soiler in the '40's and '50's.[2] Is Donald implying that Free Soilism also can be explained to some extent by the "status revolution" concept? It is impossible to answer this question from the essay.

In short, Donald's essay does not answer several questions crucial to the validity of his interpretation of abolitionism. His essay is entitled "Toward a Reconsideration of Abolitionists," but it attempts only to deal with one segment of abolitionists, the leaders. More specifically, it relates to 106 leaders only; the criteria of leaders are that the individuals were genuine abolitionists during the 1830's and not "advocates of colonizing the freed Negroes in Africa" nor individuals having "only incidental interests or sympathy for emancipation." Names of the 106 abolitionists are not given, and no information is supplied as to where they resided. Though Donald says the 106 leaders were abolitionists in the 1830's, the essay fails to clarify whether it concerns only abolitionists of the 1830's or includes wartime abolitionists who were neither abolitionists in the 1830's nor Free-Soilers in the 1840's.

Even if these problems were clarified, however, and even if Donald had supplied the names of the 106 individuals, one further question of historical method would remain: What types of evidence

2 Charles Francis Adams, *Richard Henry Dana, a Biography* (2 vols., Boston, 1890), I, 122–126.

are necessary to establish with reasonable certainty a "social interpretation" of the rise of abolitionism before 1840? Clearly, one type of necessary evidence is that which Donald has attempted to present, that is, evidence showing that individual abolitionists (leaders or followers) possessed the specified social background. But would it not be desirable or perhaps necessary to present a second type of evidence, evidence showing by comparison that other individuals did *not* have the same social background as the abolitionists? For if nonabolitionists (in proportionate numbers) came from social backgrounds identical to the backgrounds of the abolitionists studied by Donald, the social background could not logically be *the determining* factor in the rise of abolitionism before 1840 and might not be even *an important* factor. Thus, until the social backgrounds of nonabolitionists (or of the population as a whole) are studied and compared with the social backgrounds of abolitionists, one cannot establish that social background was *an important* factor in explaining the rise of abolitionism before 1840.

One specific example of the dangers involved in drawing conclusions from the social backgrounds of abolitionists without first making a comparison with the backgrounds of nonabolitionists is Donald's statement concerning the rural nature of the abolitionist movement. His analysis of the 106 leaders showed that "only thirteen of the entire group were born in any of the principal cities of the United States." Disregarding the problem of defining a principal city, the descriptive statement is clear. Approximately twelve per cent of the abolitionist leaders were born in principal cities. As eighty-eight per cent were therefore not born in principal cities, Donald concludes that

"Abolition was distinctly a rural movement. . . ."

The census reports do not record how many individuals were *born* in cities, nor, of course, do they record how many individuals were leaders of social movements; but when the abolitionist leaders are compared with the *general population* living in cities it is seen not only that Donald's conclusion is unwarranted, but that indeed the opposite conclusion might be drawn. . . . In 1790, out of a total population of 3,929,214 there were 157,404 living in the twelve cities with populations over 5,000. That is, only slightly more than *four* per cent of the total population resided in the twelve largest cities, while approximately twelve per cent of the 106 abolitionist leaders were born in principal cities. In 1810, out of a total population of 7,223,787 there were 455,688 in the twenty-eight cities over 5,000.[3] In other words, slightly over six per cent of the total population lived in the twenty-eight largest cities, while twelve per cent of Donald's 106 abolitionists were born in "principal" cities. The conclusion seems to be that the percentage of the 106 abolitionist leaders born in cities was considerably higher than the percentage of the total population living in cities in 1790 or 1810.

Donald has probed to new psychological and sociological depths in articulating a social interpretation to explain the rise of abolitionism in the 1830's. But the interpretation as presented is not clear in some important respects, nor does it present the comparative evidence necessary to establish the thesis.

[3] The census figures are taken from *Historical Statistics of the United States, 1789–1945, a Supplement to the Statistical Abstract of the United States* (Washington, 1949), 26, 29.

MARTIN B. DUBERMAN (1930–   ), assistant professor of American history at Princeton University, agrees with Donald and others that the methods and insights of allied academic disciplines—sociology, psychology, and cultural anthropology—can increase our knowledge and understanding of abolitionism and other reform movements. However, he finds that historians have thus far oversimplified the application of interdisciplinary methods to historical problems.*

The Abolitionists and Psychology

Out of their heightened concern with the pressing question of Negro rights, a number of historians, especially the younger ones, have begun to take a new look at the abolitionists, men who in their own day were involved in a similar movement of social change. About both them and ourselves we are asking anew such questions as the proper role of agitation, the underlying motives of both reformers and resistants, and the useful limits of outside interference. From this questioning a general tendency has developed to view the abolitionists in a more favorable light than previously. As yet, however, it is a tendency only,

and hostility to the abolitionists continues to be strong among historians.

Perhaps one reason why no fuller re-evaluation has taken place is that historians have been made cautious by the fate of previous "revisionist" scholarship. We have seen how current preoccupations can prompt dubious historical re-evaluations. But this need not always be the case. Contemporary pressures, if recognized and contained, can prove fruitful in stimulating the historical imagination. This may lead us to uncover (not invent) aspects of the past to which we were previously blind.

If historians need more courage in

their re-consideration of the abolitionists, they also need more information. Particularly do they need to employ some of the insights and raise some of the questions which developments in related fields of knowledge have made possible. Recent trends in psychology seem especially pertinent, though historians have not paid them sufficient attention. It is my hope in this paper to make some beginning in that direction.

It might be well to start by referring to one of psychology's older principles, the uniqueness of personality. Each individual, with his own genetic composition and his own life experience, will develop into a distinctive organism. There are, of course, certain drives and reflexes which are more or less "instinctive." There are also a variety of common responses conditioned by our membership in a particular group, be it family, class, church or nation. These similarities among human beings make possible the disciplines of sociology, anthropology and social psychology, which concern themselves with patterns of behavior, and demonstrate that no man is *sui generis*. But it does not follow that the qualities which are uniquely individual are mere irrelevancies. As Gordon Allport has said, ". . . all of the animals in the world are psychologically less distinct from one another than one man is from other men."

This is not to question, of course, the validity of attempts, whether they be by sociologists, psychologists or historians, to find meaningful similarities in the behavioral patterns of various human groups. The point is to make certain that such similarities genuinely exist, and further, to be aware that in describing them, we do not pretend to be saying everything about the individuals involved. Historians, it seems, are prone to

ignore both cautions—their treatment of the abolitionists being the immediate case in point.

With barely a redeeming hint of uncertainty, many historians list a group of "similar traits" which are said to characterize all abolitionists: "impractical," "self-righteous," "fanatical," "humorless," "vituperative," and,—if they are very modern in their terminology—"disturbed." The list varies, but usually only to include adjectives equally hostile and denunciatory. The stereotype of the "abolitionist personality," though fluid in details, is clear enough in its general outlines.

But did most abolitionists really share these personality traits? The fact is, we know much less about the individuals involved in the movement than has been implied. Some of the major figures, such as Joshua Leavitt, have never received biographical treatment; others—the Tappans, Edmund Quincy, and Benjamin Lundy, for example—badly need modern appraisal. And the careers and personalities of the vast majority of significant secondary figures—people like Lydia Maria Child, Sidney Gay, Maria Weston Chapman, Henry B. Stanton, and Abby Kelley Foster—have been almost totally unexplored. Whence comes the confidence, then, that allows historians to talk of "the abolitionist personality," as if this had been microscopically examined and painstakingly reconstructed?

Certainly the evidence which we do have, does not support such confident theorizing. In order to adhere to this conceptual strait-jacket, it is necessary to ignore or discount much that conflicts with it—the modesty of Theodore Weld, the wit of James Russell Lowell, the tender humanity of Whittier, the worldly charm of Edmund Quincy. This does not mean that we need leap to the opposite extreme and claim all abolitionists were saints and seraphs. But if some of them were disagreeable or disturbed, we want, instead of a blanket indictment, to know which ones and in what ways; we want some recognition of the variety of human beings who entered the movement.

It seems to me that what too many historians have done is to take William Lloyd Garrison as a personality symbol for the entire movement (at the same time, ironically, that they deny him the commanding leadership which he was once assumed to have had). Fixing on some of the undeniably "neurotic" aspects of his personality (and bolstered, it should be said, by the eccentric psychographs of other abolitionists—a Gerrit Smith say, or a Stephen Foster), they equate these with the personality structures of all the abolitionists, and conclude that the movement was composed solely of "quacks." In doing so, they fail to do justice to the wide spectrum of personality involved; in fact, they do not even do justice to Garrison, for to speak exclusively of *his* oracular and abusive qualities is to ignore the considerable evidence of personal warmth and kindliness.

It may be that when we know more of other abolitionists, we may with equal certainty be able to single out qualities in them which seem palpable symptoms of "disturbance." But let the evidence at least precede the judgment. And let us also show a decent timidity in applying the label "neurotic." Psychiatrists, dealing with a multitude of evidence and bringing to it professional insights, demonstrate more caution in this regard than do untrained historians working with mere traces of personality. If the disposition to be hostile exists, "neurosis" can almost always be established. Under the Freudian microscope, it would be a rare man indeed whose life showed no evidence of pathological behavior. (Think, for one, of the admirable William James, who, as his devoted biographer, Ralph Barton Perry, has shown, was subject to hypochondria, hallucinations, and intense oscillations of mood.) I am not suggesting that all men's lives, if sufficiently investigated, would show equally severe evidence of disturbance. I mean only to warn that, given the double jeopardy of a hostile commentator and the weight of a hostile historical tradition, we must take special precaution not to be too easily convinced by the "evidence" of neurosis in the abolitionists.

And even were we to establish the neurotic component of behavior, the story would certainly not be complete. To know the pathological elements in an individual's behavior is not to know everything about his behavior. To say that Garrison, in his fantasy world, longed to be punished and thus deliberately courted martyrdom, or that Wendell Phillips, alienated from the "new order," sought to work out his private grievances against the industrial system by indirectly attacking it through slavery is hardly to exhaust their range of possible motives. We know far too little about why men do anything—let alone why they do something as specific as joining a reform movement—to assert as confidently as historians have, the motives of whole groups of men. We may never know enough about the human psyche to achieve a comprehensive analysis of motivation; how much greater the difficulty when the subject is dead and we are attempting the analysis on the basis of partial and fragmentary remains.

Our best hope for increased understanding in this area—aside from the artist's tool of intuition—is in the researches of psychology. But at present there is no agreed-upon theory of motivation among psychologists. Gordon Allport, however, summarizing current opinion, suggests that behavior does not result solely from the need to reduce tension, but may also aim (especially in a "healthy" person) at distant goals, the achievement of which can be gained only by maintaining tension. Allport does not press his views, realizing the complexity of the problems at issue. But his hypotheses are at least suggestive as regards the abolitionists, for their motives, rather than being solely the primitive ones of eliminating personal tension (under the guise of ethical commitment), may also have included a healthy willingness to bear tension (in the form of ostracism, personal danger and material sacrifice) in order to persevere in pursuit of long-range ideals.

Acceptance of these suggestions runs into the massive resistance of neo-Freudian cynicism. How old-fashioned, it will be said, to talk in terms of "ideals" or "conscience," since these are only unconscious rationalizations for "darker" drives which we are unable to face. How old-fashioned, too, to talk as if men could exercise choice in their conduct, since all our behavior is determined by our antecedents.

But the surprising fact is that such views are not old-fashioned. On the contrary, they have recently returned to favor in psychoanalytical circles. Increasing dissatisfaction with the ability of behaviorist theory fully to explain human action, has led to a reconsideration of the role of reason and the possibilities of purposive, deliberate behavior. The result is the influential new school of "ego

psychology," which views man as endowed with a considerable margin of freedom and responsibility, and which has restored to the vocabulary such "old fashioned" terminology as character, willpower and conscience. Moral earnestness, moreover, is no longer equated with self-deception. As Allport has said, the very mark of maturity "seems to be the range and extent of one's feeling of self-involvement in abstract ideals." Some of these new emphases had been prefigured in the work of such philosophers as Sartre, who have long stressed social action as a sign of "authenticity" in man.

But although all of this makes a re-evaluation of the abolitionists possible, it does not make one necessary. Men may now be thought capable of impersonal devotion to ideals, but this does not mean that the abolitionists were such men. Maturity may now be defined as the ability to commit ourselves objectively to ethical values, but it does not follow that every man who makes such a commitment does so out of mature motives.

Yet at least some doubts should be raised in our minds as to whether we have been fair in regarding the abolitionists as psychologically homogeneous, and at that, homogeneous in the sense of being self-deceived. My own feeling goes beyond doubt, into conviction. I do not claim, to repeat, that because the abolitionists fought in a noble cause, their motives were necessarily noble—i.e., "pure" and "unselfish," unrelated in any way to their own inner turmoil and conflicts. A connection between inner problems and outer convictions probably always exists to some degree. But an individual's public involvement is never completely explained by discussing his private pathology. Yet it is just this that historians have frequently done, and to that degree, they have distorted and de-valued the abolitionist commitment.

To provide a concrete example, by way of summary, consider the case of James Russell Lowell, whose biography I am writing, and about whom I can talk with more assurance than I might some other figure.

His history seems to me convincing proof that at least some people became abolitionists not primarily out of an un-conscious need to escape from personal problems, but out of a deliberate, ration-al commitment to certain ethical values —recognizing that the two are never wholly unrelated. Lowell's active life as a reformer came during the period of his greatest contentment—secure in a supremely happy marriage, and confi-dent of his talents and his future. His contemporaries agree in describing him as a gay, witty, warm man, without seri-ous tensions or disabling anxieties. I have come across so little evidence of "pathology" in the Lowell of these years that when the standard picture of the abolitionist as a warped eccentric is applied to him, it becomes absurd.

And he *was* an abolitionist, though various arguments have been used to deny this. Lowell, it has been said, came to the movement late—and only at the instigation of his bride, Maria White, who was a confirmed reformer; he never fully committed himself to abolition, and finally left the ranks in the early 1850's. There may be some justice to these charges, but on the whole the argument is not persuasive. Given Lowell's youth (he was born in 1819) he could not have joined the movement much earlier than he did (which was around 1840), and there is evidence that he was involved in the cause before he met Maria White. The important point is that for roughly

ten years he was unquestionably a serious abolitionist, both as an active member of the Massachusetts Anti-Slavery Society, and as a frequent contributor to aboli-tionist periodicals. The reasons for his drifting out of the movement are com-plex, but turn largely on the fact that his wife's death in 1853 destroyed the struc-ture of his life and left him apathetic to public issues. (Might not this give added weight to the argument that it takes a reasonably contented man to interest himself in the problems of others?)

Even when it is admitted that Lowell was an abolitionist, he is dismissed as not having been a "typical" one. But who was the typical abolitionist? Is the stand-ard of measurement meant to be some outstanding individual—Garrison, say, or Theodore Weld—and is everyone else to be considered more or less of an aboli-tionist depending on how closely he ap-proximated the personality structure of the model? But a man may be prom-inent in a movement without necessarily typifying it. And which of several leading —and very different—figures should be chosen as the model? The decision is likely to be arbitrary (and unconscious), varying with each historian.

Or is the standard of measurement meant to be some composite group of traits which accurately describe the large number of abolitionists, so that when any single individual fails to exhibit these traits, he may justifiably be dismissed as "the exception which proves the rule?" This approach is more reasonable, but here again we run up against the old difficulty of drawing a genuinely valid group portrait. We know so little about the individual personalities and careers of the majority of abolitionists that it seems like putting the cart before the horse to even talk about a composite

portrait. Certainly the one which is now
commonly accepted ("impractical"; "self-
righteous," etc.) fails adequately to describe many of the abolitionists about
whom we do have information. I mean
here not only Lowell, but a number of
others. What I have seen in my researches
into the papers of people like Edmund
Quincy, Lydia Maria Child or Maria
Weston Chapman (to name only a few
of the more prominent), has created the
strong suspicion in my mind that if their
personalities were to be investigated in
depth, they too would be found to de-
viate from the accepted portrait in so
many significant ways as further to un-
dermine its reliability.

A conceptual scheme may yet be devised which adequately describes the motives and actions of most of the abolitionists. But if so, it will not be of the primitive kind thus far suggested. There is no
reason why historians cannot legitimately
investigate group patterns, but to do so
meaningfully, they must become skilled
in the techniques of sociology and other
related disciplines. This takes time and
inclination, and the historian, busy with
his special interests and orientated towards the particular, rarely has either.
Unfortunately this does not always prevent him from trying his hand, though
the result has too often been the kind

of elementary categorizing used to describe the abolitionists.

Opinions will continue to differ as to
the best way of achieving desired social
change. Our own generation's confronta-
tion with segregation has made this clear.
Many of us feel as strongly about the
evil of that practice as the abolitionists
did about the institution of slavery. Like
them, too, we have scant faith in Southern voluntarism or the benevolent workings of time; patience and inactivity have
not done their work. Naturally we would
like to believe that our sense of urgency
comes from concern for the Negro rather
than from a need to escape from some
private torment of our own. Because of
this we are admittedly prone to credit
our historical counterparts with the kind
of good motives we would like to impute
to ourselves. Our wish to think well of
them may account for our doing so. But
as Erich Fromm has said, "the fact that
an idea satisfies a wish does not mean
necessarily that the idea is false." There
is much in the new psychology to encourage the belief that the idea is not
false. At any rate, if we are to find out,
we need less dogma, more research, and a
chastening sense of wonder at the complexities of human nature.

FRANK THISTLETHWAITE (1915–   ),
Vice Chancellor of the University of East Anglia,
Norwich, England, here develops the thesis,
formulated earlier by Gilbert H. Barnes, that
American abolitionists were largely indebted
to British antislavery radicals for their methods
and ideas.*

The Movement Derived Largely from England

The [British] antislavery lobby succeeded in 1833 in forcing the Government to introduce a bill which, though not altogether to their liking, abolished slavery in the West Indies.

However, the antislavery zealots by no means rested on their oars. Slavery must now be abolished throughout the world, and especially, where it loomed blackest, in the United States. For had not John Wesley on his deathbed written to Wilberforce, "Go on, in the Name of God and in the power of His might, till even American slavery, the vilest that ever saw the sun, shall vanish away before you"?

West Indian emancipation caught the imagination of kindred spirits in the United States. In 1833 antislavery sentiment was still canalized into the American Colonization Society's scheme, supported by slaveholders, for exporting free and freed Negroes to Liberia. Only a handful had followed along the British path from gradual emancipation (and emigration), to immediate abolition and of these, William Lloyd Garrison, who had recently launched the *Liberator* and the New England Anti-Slavery Society, was a lonely, if strident, voice. The West India Emancipation Act not only gave heart to incipient abolitionists, but provided them with a plan of action. American abolitionists never tired of proclaim-

* Reprinted without footnotes from *The Anglo-American Connection in the Early Nineteenth Century* by Frank Thistlethwaite, by permission of the University of Pennsylvania Press. Copyright © 1959 by the Trustees of the University of Pennsylvania. Pp. 107–119.

ing their debt to the British movement. "The abolition movement in America," said the ex-slave, Frederick Douglass, "was largely derived from England," adding later, with characteristic American reservations, "surely in this sense it ought to be no disgrace to be an Englishman, even on the soil of the freest people on the globe." August 1, Emancipation Day, was annually celebrated in antislavery circles until the Civil War, with warm expressions of amity towards Britain.

The Emancipation Act prompted Arthur Tappan, Joshua Leavitt and Henry C. Wright in the same year to form the American Anti-Slavery Society in Philadelphia self-consciously on the British model. Even before the bill was passed the importunate Garrison had appeared in London to solicit support from the British society for the American cause and to counteract the fund-raising efforts of Elliott Cresson, emissary of the hated American Colonization Society. While in London, where he breakfasted with the antislavery chiefs-of-staff, and walked behind Wilberforce's bier to Westminster Abbey, Garrison decided that what the cause especially needed in America was the services of the ace agitator George Thompson, and he determined to import him. Some of the more conservative British leaders like Clarkson and Sturge were dubious about the propriety of so direct an intervention in the affairs of another country. However, like other antislavery zealots, Garrison and Thompson, who became lifelong friends, were fanatics who recognized no barriers, international or domestic, to moral agitation.

"In moral questions, I say, there are no nations," said Phillips. "Our country is the world, our countrymen are all mankind. We love the land of our nativity only as we love all other lands," affirmed Garrison; and Thompson said, "Ours is a peaceful remonstrance with America for her sins. . . . We resort . . . but to moral influence." In the delicate question of importing British influence into the United States, all would have seconded Frederick Douglass when he said:

the growing intercourse between England and this country by means of steam-navigation . . . gives us an opportunity to bring in the aid . . . of those living on the other side of the Atlantic. . . . We entreat our British friends to continue to send in their remonstrances across the deep against slavery in this land.

Sharing such sentiments, Thompson was not squeamish about using his powerful gifts to stir up in a foreign country an issue which threatened the balance of society and politics at its most delicate point.

English vistors to the United States were curious about slavery, even to the lengths of a morbid fascination with slave auctions. But although a minority, like the Mrs. Maury who was concerned about the servant problem, were in favor of the institution, most were hostile. If the stray remarks of a traveling bookseller could earn him a whipping in Virginia in 1832, and those of an English actor could attract an antislavery mob to the Bowery Theatre in 1834, the advent of an English antislavery agitator in the same year was bound to bring trouble. George Thompson's visit to the United States, in 1834-5, ended with his ignominious exit by rowing [a] boat to a New Brunswick-bound brig. By his rhetorical gifts, and his tactless energy he succeeded, almost singlehanded, in provoking the first great wave of Southern bitterness against Northern interference, and in giving the antislavery movement a foreign and alien character. He became, indeed, so notorious as to be the object of a reference in President Jackson's Message to Congress to "emissaries from foreign parts who have dared to interfere in this matter." But in the narrow sense he did much for the cause. He saved the *Liberator* from extinction; his exposure to mob violence in New England provided a new object of hero worship for those with the temperament of martyrs; and during his indefatigable journeys and speeches, he did for the Northeastern States what he had done for Britain. His visit coincided with a phenomenal growth in local antislavery societies, which numbered five hundred by 1835; and it seems likely that his oratory, in over two hundred addresses, was responsible for several hundreds of these auxiliaries which, like their British counterparts, were federated to the national antislavery society, held meetings and fund-raising fairs, distributed tracts, and drafted petitions to state legislatures and Congress. In all this activity, British influence was paramount. When John Quincy Adams embarked on his brilliant, political second childhood as the abolitionist Congressman from Massachusetts responsible for presenting antislavery petitions he was accused of being in league with British abolitionists.

After Thompson's departure, the American Anti-Slavery Society carried its organization a stage further in the direction of the British model. In 1837 it set up an Agency Committee, not of six like the British Committee, but, with Yankee exuberance, of seventy paid antislavery lecturers. The director of "The Seventy" was Theodore Weld, late of the Lane Seminary, who had been converted

to abolition by another British evangelical, Captain Charles Stuart. Stuart had returned to the United States in 1834 slightly ahead of Thompson, armed with a presentation to Prudence Crandall from British antislavery ladies and with one thousand dollars for a manual labor school in New Haven. He was an eccentric character. An officer in the East India Company service, he had fought under Wellington, and had retired to Canada, and later to western New York, where he had taught school. He was a strange figure who "wore on all occasions and at all seasons a Scotch plaid frock with a cape reaching nearly to his elbows." At Utica, in 1824, he was converted by Brother Finney to evangelical Christianity, and there he befriended the young Theodore Weld, putting him through the Oneida Institute and concerning himself passionately with his spiritual welfare. In 1829 Stuart went to England on temperance matters, there became converted to antislavery, and, like Thompson, was made a lecturer for the British Agency Committee. His pamphlets, *The West India Question,* and *Thoughts on African Colonization,* proved a powerful influence in the United States in favor of immediate abolition and against gradualism. He was instrumental in converting Weld to the antislavery cause.... He spent the following thirty years flitting between Canada, the United States, and the British Isles in various good works, including relief during the Irish famine, and toward the end of his life helped finance John Brown's campaign in Kansas.

The violence offered to the abolition cause, in the persons of Thompson, Garrison, Stuart, and others even in the North created a sensation in British antislavery circles. The story was brought home to them by Harriet Martineau in her *Westminster Review* account which she called "The Martyr Age in the United States"; for she had seen the mob assembling in Boston to tar and feather Garrison and Thompson, and had subsequently been forced by conscience, and perhaps a personal yearning for martyrdom, to declare herself an abolitionist, at some expense to her American connections.... As early as the year of Emancipation, Joseph Sturge had written to William Forster:

Some of my ideas, so far as they have assumed a tangible shape, are these: That a Society should be at once formed for the abolition of slavery throughout the world. . . . The effect of this example throughout the American continent will no doubt be great. . . . Let us therefore form a general crusade against this accursed system throughout the civilized world.

Six years later Sturge and others redeployed the antislavery forces as the British and Foreign Anti-Slavery Society, with no less an object than world abolition. This meant above all the abolition of American slavery. In practical terms the primary object was to co-operate with the American Anti-Slavery Society in its efforts against the institution in the Southern States. Thenceforward the two national Societies maintained close relations, reinforced by correspondence between Sturge in London and Birmingham and Lewis Tappan in New York, by the exchange of intelligence, pamphlets and newspapers, and virtually annual visits across the Atlantic. As with the sister crusades of peace and temperance, the crown of this benevolent organization was the "World Anti-Slavery Convention." Two of these largely Anglo-American affairs were held in London; the second, in 1843, was a pallid

successor to the first, more famous and important Convention, held in 1840.

June, 1840, was a moment of high excitement for the friends of the slave. There gathered in the Freemasons' Hall, Great Queen Street, between five and six hundred delegates, including not only the stalwarts of British evangelicalism but fifty-three delegates from American antislavery societies who had crossed the Atlantic to take part in such a week of debate, resolution-drafting and moral exhortation as the world of Exeter Hall had never before enjoyed. Sturge organized it; but the Americans conceived the idea and the chief object was to mobilize Anglo-American opinion against American slavery. Resolutions were passed in favor of boycotting slave-grown produce and substituting the "free" cotton of India for Lancashire's intake from the American South; but the true theme of the convention was set by the aged Clarkson whose opening speech concentrated on the conscience of the Southern planter. For what the Americans chiefly wanted was the heavy artillery of British moral support.

" I hardly exaggerate," Phillips had written to Thompson the previous year, "when I say that the sympathy and brotherly appeals of British Christians are the sheet anchor of our cause" and, to underline the authority which Britain still exercised in the intellectual and moral realms, he went on:

England . . . is the fountain-head of our literature; the slightest censure, every argument, every rebuke on the pages of your reviews, strikes on the ear of the remotest dweller in our country. . . . In the name of the slave, I beseech you, let literature speak out, in deep, stern and indignant tones.

This argument was repeated at the Convention by Henry B. Stanton who considered the British reviews the best means of bringing the opinion of the civilized world into the South. It permeated the debates.

This effort to mobilize opinion against slavery concentrated on the Churches. The Americans hoped to shame the South by isolating her from the Christian community, and they were worried about the fraternal relations, cemented by some recent transatlantic visits, between British denominations and their co-religionists in the South. Pressure was therefore brought to bear on the Churches to withhold membership from slaveholders. Resolutions to this effect were transmitted to the leading British and American denominations; and Clarkson in his eightieth year was prompted to write his *Letters to the Clergy of the Various Denominations and to the Slave-holding Planters in the Southern Parts of the United States.* The chief Non-conformist Churches in Britain—the Wesleyan Methodist Conference, the Congregational Union, and the Baptist Union—did their duty that same summer; and during the next few years the Churches held to their antislavery position, which was reinforced in 1846 by the British branch of the Evangelical Alliance. But the subject remained controversial, as was seen in 1844 in the case of the newly formed Free Church of Scotland which had need, financial and moral, of close liaison with the American Presbyterian Church in the South as well as in the North.

Approaching the American denominations was a more delicate matter. Even the Society of Friends, though committed to antislavery, shrank from radical abolition, and proved a sorrow to their more militant members, especially in Britain where their scruples were not understood. English Friends were shocked to discover that colored people were segregated in Meeting, and concerned at the lack of response to hortatory minutes sent to American Meetings. A tactful epistle to North Carolina Friends ran: "We can sympathise with you in your difficulties and trials on (the slaves') behalf but we hope that you will not be weary in welldoing." Joseph Sturge's third object in visiting the United States the year after the Convention was to stir American Friends on the issue. The Unitarians, also, though finally approving such a resolution in 1844, considered a memorial from the British Unitarians as an impertinence. As for the major denominations, the slavery conflict which led in the case of the Methodists and Baptists to schisms between Northern and Southern churches in 1842 and 1845, was exacerbated by the resolutions of the World Anti-Slavery Convention of 1840.

However, the most striking fact about the Convention was the changed temper of the Anglo-American connection on slavery. Henry B. Stanton expressed it when he told the Convention, "To be an abolitionist in England and in America are very different things; and if I may be permitted to say so, but a few of your abolitionists have stood the fire on our side of the Atlantic." Five years earlier British antislavery men and women had stood the fire. Since then, however, an American generation of radical abolitionists had been exposed to implications of conscience far beyond British experience. After all, Exeter Hall was to survive in the Strand until the twentieth century; but Pennsylvania Hall in Philadelphia had been burnt down within a few days of its dedication by a howling proslavery mob. Harriet Martineau experienced the contrast in tension. "When I returned home," she wrote, "the daily feeling of security and of sympathy in my antislavery views gave me a pleasure as intense as if I had returned from a long exile, instead of a tour of recreation." To be an abolitionist in Boston, Philadelphia or Cincinnati meant courting social ostracism, business ruin and physical assault: it called for qualities of personal courage and character which should not be minimized, however, foolhardy and short-sighted the single-mindedness which went with it. For Americans, slavery was in the back yard and the color problem in the kitchen and the meeting house. In American eyes, British antislavery was drawing room philanthropy. As one American wrote home to his wife: "These anti-slavery men do not burn with the fire of real enthusiasm like that of our own faithful and sterling friends. Their emancipation is but a political, parliamentary one. It has no heart in it compared with ours." In British eyes, he and his fellow American delegates in London had the glamor, if not of martyrs, of front-line fighters with personal experience of slavery and persecution. For drawing room philanthropists, Garrison was a celebrity, and ex-slaves like Remond and, later, others like Douglass, were objects of devout lionizing. In England's Romantic Age they represented the Savage who had only to be released from his chains to become a free and noble man. . . .

The great majority of British evangelicals, led by Sturge and the Quakers, wishing to keep strictly to antislavery, held aloof from Garrison's "April's Fool" party, and for the next twenty years remained loyal to the conservative, so-called "New Organization," the American and Foreign Anti-Slavery Society.

But a few of the more intellectually lively, including those like Harriet Martineau who were not evangelical and others of a younger generation who were beginning to react against the narrow piety of their fathers, responded to the magnetism of Garrison and his universalist ideas. The Garrisonians, therefore, continued to enjoy a hearing in Britain, and representatives like John A. Collins spent some time traveling and raising funds there. A portrait of Garrison had an honored place in Harriet Martineau's library at Ambleside.

However, 1840 proved to be the high-watermark of Anglo-American agitation against slavery. For one thing philanthropic agitation, like many things in that hard Victorian world, depended on the trade cycle, and by 1841 the evangelical bankers and merchants whose golden guineas and dollars had financed it were hard-pressed by the stringencies of depression. But apart from this, where could a movement based on moral exhortation go after a world convention? . . . The British and American societies collaborated during the forties to lobby Foreign Office and State Department on such issues as the protection of fugitive slaves in Canada and Negro seamen in Southern and West Indian ports, as in the *Amistad* and *Creole* cases. The British antislavery lobby supported the Aberdeen Government in its attempt to maintain Texan independence, in the hope of preserving that State from the full blight of Southern slavery; but such were the limits imposed by nationalism upon Anglo-American opinion that rumors of British intervention only served to overcome Northern resistance to annexation. The concrete results of the 1840 demonstration of sentiment were not impressive.

More practical spirits in each country sensed this, and turned their energies towards linking antislavery to broader political issues: in Britain to the radical attack on the establishment through Chartism or the Anti-Corn Law League, in the United States to an attack on the South by aligning sectional interests, North and West, against it. In both countries the inexorable demands of domestic politics and society pulled the Atlantic movement apart. Henceforward, although the two antislavery societies collaborated, the Garrisonians conducting a bitter guerrilla warfare on the side, the effervescence had subsided, the belief that immediate wonders could be performed by the holding up of hands, had waned.

And yet this Anglo-American movement had perhaps accomplished more than appeared. Whatever the role of abolitionists in America in bringing about the alignment which led to civil war, the antislavery movement in Britain had made popular opinion aware of the evils of American slavery.

THOMAS F. HARWOOD (1919–   ), assistant
professor of American history at Louisiana State
University, New Orleans, discusses the effects of
direct pressures exerted by British abolitionists
on American churches during the 1830s. He maintains
that although historians have recognized that schisms
in American churches "helped to bring on secession
and war," they have not "fully appreciated the
importance of British influence in producing
these divisions."*

British Evangelicalism a Divisive
Influence on Protestant Churches

In his sad valedictory speech during
the debates over the Compromise of 1850,
John C. Calhoun compared the major
Protestant denominations to cords of
union. He warned that the rupture of
some and tension in others resulting
from the slavery issue portended federal
dissolution. Historians since have generally agreed that divisions in the
churches greatly weakened the national
structure and helped to bring on secession and war; but historians have not
always appreciated the importance of
pressures from British evangelical abolitionism as contributing causes to the ex-
plosions in American churches.[1]

The exchange of antislavery impulses

between British and American churches
occurred almost from the outset of the
English-speaking antislavery movement.
Indeed, the earliest significant development of the movement, in the middle of
the eighteenth century, has been described as a transatlantic ground swell of
British and American Quakers. . . .

But British antislavery religious groups
exerted their greatest influence on Amer-

[1] I use the descriptive term *evangelical* because the pressures were primarily evangelical in
character. They emanated from the more evangelical elements in British Protestantism, insisted
upon an evangelical conception of slavery as a
dangerous sin, and urged an application of
evangelical techniques in the campaign for its
eradication.

* From Thomas F. Harwood, "British Evangelical Abolitionism and American Churches in the
1830's," *Journal of Southern History*, XXVIII (August, 1962), 287–306. Reprinted with most of
the footnotes omitted by permission of the managing editor of the *Journal of Southern History*.
Copyright © 1962 by the Southern Historical Association.

ican churches in the 1830's. Earlier, they had been mainly concerned with the drive against bondage in an area where they felt direct responsibility—the British West Indies. Upon achievement of emancipation for the islands' Negroes in 1833, many of the British evangelicals were ready to lend what support they could to the renascent American antislavery movement.

American abolitionists were eager for support from British religious groups. In 1835 the secretary of the New England Anti-Slavery Society sent a circular to leading divines in London, Glasgow, and Edinburgh, requesting that British Christians join with some of the American churches in a special day of fasting and prayer for the slaves. When the American Anti-Slavery Society later set aside the last Monday in every month as such a day, it requested British churches to send their prayers to Heaven on those days. It also warmly commended antislavery letters from British to American churches. . . . Apologists for slavery, realizing the danger of abolitionist infiltration of the churches, pointed out that the great English antislavery patriarchs, William Wilberforce and Thomas Clarkson, had made little headway until British ministers busied themselves in the cause and warned that an English preacher, the Rev. F. A. Cox, was urging American churches to follow the example of British churches by assuming leadership in the antislavery movement, since "deliverance must come out of Zion."

The Baptist and Methodist churches, the two largest denominations in America, reacted similarly in the 1830's to the stimulus of the new abolitionism. British Baptists and Methodists contributed to the antislavery stimulus by exerting direct pressure upon their American co-

religionists. The majority in both denominations in America resentfully rejected this outside interference, but the end result was increased dissension within each church and a notable increase in antislavery strength among Northern members. The stage was set for the sectional split of both churches over the slavery issue in the next decade. American Presbyterians and Quakers did not follow exactly the same pattern in their antislavery crusade of the 1830's, and their British counterparts did not apply antislavery pressure in exactly the same way as did the British Methodists and Baptists. But again British evangelical abolitionism helped to build up tension and divisive forces inside the American churches.

British Baptists, although the most loosely organized among major denominations, were among the most forward in pressing their American brethren about slavery. Soon after emancipation in the West Indies, the Board of Baptist Ministers In and Near London addressed the "Pastors and Ministers of the Baptist Denominations Throughout the United States." Recalling the role of Baptists in the British antislavery triumph and pointing out that as soon as a proper Christian appeal had been made to the British nation slavery in the West Indies was brought to an end, they "conceived" that American Christians had only "to act in the spirit and with the firmness of Christian principle" in order to accomplish what British Christians had achieved. To this appeal the Baptist Board of Foreign Missions in America sent a lengthy reply, pointing out that Congress had no power over the states such as that of Parliament over the West Indies, that the number of slaves and the character of the institution in the United

States made the problem one of "appalling difficulty" and that the course recommended by the British would disrupt the "pleasing degree of union among the multiplying thousands of Baptists throughout our land." A dissenting letter dispatched from a Baptist convention in Boston, however, promised to accept the British advice. The Boston convention maintained that the United States could not be exonerated from the sin of slavery on the ground of the powers reserved to the states as slavery in the District of Columbia and in the territories was under national protection. . . . Thus, a British antislavery message provoked in 1833–34 controversially different responses within a major American denomination.

The British Baptist Union greatly intensified the rising controversy between abolitionist-minded Baptists and conservative Baptists in the United States by sending over a special deputation to attend the triennial convention of American Baptist bodies in 1835. . . . Antislavery had high priority among the messages to be delivered to the American Brethren, and the deputies were chosen for their zeal in that cause. One of them, the Rev. F. A. Cox, was a member of the Agency Society for the Universal Abolition of Negro Slavery. Moreover, the circular used to raise money for the expenses of the deputation had promised that the deputies would "most zealously . . . promote the cause of Negro emancipation."

The triennial convention, unfortunately for the Britishers' purposes, met that year in Richmond, Virginia. Cox and his fellow deputy, the Rev. J. H. Hoby, were called aside by leading American Baptists, Northern and Southern, before the sessions began. When time came for the Britons to deliver their messages, they made no allusions to their antislavery sentiments.

Shortly after the Richmond Conference, Cox was in New York, where he had planned to attend the May anniversary meeting of the American Anti-Slavery Society. When the convention began, however, he did not appear, sending instead a note which explained that his absence was due not to any lack of feeling on the subject of slavery but to an awareness that the case had "political bearings" in America which he had not before realized. He declared that it now seemed to him impertinent for a foreigner to "intermeddle" in the matter. Later it was unkindly pointed out that though both he and George Thompson, a flamboyant British abolitionist then touring the North, had been warned by placards and the press not to attend the convention, Thompson, unlike Cox, went anyway and addressed the convention.

In his address, Thompson charged that the "torpedo power" of the American slavocracy had struck dumb a man who had been eloquent in England. He pointed out that, in contrast to Cox, he himself made the same speeches before hostile American crowds as he had made before admiring throngs in Exeter Hall, the great London sounding board of nineteenth-century philanthropic causes. Finally Thompson's remarks about both Cox and American "conspiracies" in favor of slavery grew so insulting that even in the antislavery convocation scattered cries against "the foreigner" were heard. Soon after the convention, Cox hurried northward, and, as if to make amends for his silence in Richmond and in New York, he proposed at a Baptist meeting in New Hampshire resolutions favoring immediate emancipation.

A storm of controversy over the conduct of Cox and Hoby broke in the Baptist world. The president of the Richmond convention, Spencer H. Cone of New York, wrote a letter defending his part in the silencing of Cox and Hoby. If Englishmen "knew that the question now presented, is equivalent to the question 'shall the Union be dissolved?' " he declared, "they would see that foreigners could not safely enter upon its discussion." Baptists all over America took sides, but a majority thought that the convention had been wise to silence the Britons and that Cox's conduct in Richmond and New York had been proper. In Great Britain, reactions were much less favorable to Cox and Hoby. George Thompson publicized the affair while touring the kingdom in 1836, and numerous letters abused Cox and Hoby for betraying the antislavery trust committed to them. At a large gathering of Baptists in Birmingham, Hoby was "arraigned and censured," and the group passed an ominous resolution, the substance of which was that every slaveholder "under any circumstances, ought to be excluded from Christian communion." Thereafter such strong antislavery messages flowed out to America from British Baptist bodies that the three American delegates chosen at the Richmond convention to represent American Baptists at the 1836 gathering of the British Baptist Union decided not to go. Two of them were slaveholders.

In 1836 Thomas Price and other Baptists in the London area founded a periodical, *Slavery in America*, which was designed to keep all British denominations posted on bondage and assaults upon it in the United States and to encourage them to send antislavery re-

monstrances to their American counterparts. Among the flood of responses to Price's appeal, one interesting specimen from the Leicestershire Association of Baptist Churches pronounced that so long as "the churches in America tolerate slavery, we must receive with great suspicion the reports which reach us of their great religious revivals." Another, coming from churches in Norwich, Lynn, Yarmouth, Dereham, Swaffham, Worsted, Aylsham, Neatishead, Ingham, Fulsham, and Cossey, disavowed fellowship and communion with American Baptist churches. From the May anniversaries of the Baptist Union of Great Britain in 1836 and 1837, long letters were dispatched to American Baptist groups. The epistles averred that slavery was a moral problem, the evasion of which no political excuses could justify, and that it was the solemn duty of the British conventions to censure American churches. . . . In May 1839, the British Baptist Union recurred to what had become an annual duty of addressing official rebukes to American churches. These British Baptist remonstrances were regularly published in the *Christian Watchman* and other American religious journals, although some of the American editors complained that none except abolitionist delegates from the United States could any longer gain admission to anniversaries of British Baptist bodies.

British Methodists had been as conspicuous as Baptists in the antislavery movement in the West Indies and in the campaign in England, and they were not behind the Baptists in turning their attention to the problem in America. The official address of the Annual Conference of British Wesleyans for 1834, just after the victory in the West Indian emancipation fight, professed regret that slavery and "sinfully degrading caste of colour" were still maintained in some Christian states and expressed hope that the example of Great Britain would be followed to wipe out the abominations. . . . In December of 1834, several prominent New England Methodist ministers, including George Storr, Jared Perkins, and La Roy Sutherland, took their cue from the British address and published an antislavery appeal to the New England conferences. The appeal quoted one of John Wesley's last letters, written to encourage the great parliamentary antislavery leader, William Wilberforce, which cited the prominent role of Methodists in the British campaign and asked why American Methodists should be "so far behind our brethren in England, in relation to this thing?" The appeal elicited a counter-appeal, probably written by the conservative Wilbur Fisk and signed by other New England Methodist preachers who shared Fisk's fears of abolitionism. The counterappeal expressed respect for British Wesleyans but pointed out the discrepancies between the position of slavery in the British Empire and in the American Union. Further, it insisted that both Wesley and Wilberforce had favored gradual emancipation, while the new American abolition societies wanted immediate, uncompensated liberation of slaves.

In 1835 the British Wesleyan Conference sent a special remonstrance to their American brethren, quoting Wesley's characterization of slavery as the "sum of all villainies" and American slavery as "the worst that ever saw the sun." The British abolitionist and Presbyterian George Thompson sought to stir up American Methodists as well as Baptists. He utilized this remonstrance and recalled the role of Methodists in the West Indies while addressing a meeting of Methodist preachers in Lynn, Massachusetts, later the same year. The Lynn meeting resulted in the formation of an antislavery organization within the New England Methodist Conference. Thompson subsequently helped organize several other Methodist antislavery societies in the conference. As contemporaries were well aware, the British messages and the work of Thompson had much to do with the fact that by 1836 a clear majority of the delegates from the New England Conference to the quadrennial General Conference of the Methodist Church were abolitionists.

When British Wesleyans injected abolitionism into the General Conference held in Cincinnati during the first fortnight of May 1836, the feverish reaction characterized by rancorous debates created much dissension. A new antislavery address from the British Wesleyan to the American General Conference reminded Americans that "great spiritual principles are opposed to the continuation of slavery in a Christian state" and urged upon American Methodists the duty of fostering a public opinion that would "result in a unanimous rejection of slavery. . . ." The Rev. Orange Scott, a presiding elder in the New England Conference who had publicly aligned himself with the antislavery cause in Boston after an inspiring speech by George Thompson, proposed that the British address be printed in the leading Methodist journals. His motion produced a "sensation" marked by angry objections from Southerns and conservatives. It was tabled.

The British Methodists had not relied solely upon a written address to the conference. They also sent an official delegate, the Rev. William Lord, who, unlike

Cox and Hoby at the Baptist convention the year before, spoke out as he had been instructed to do. He told the assembly that "the Wesleyan Methodists of England were IN TOTO opposed to slavery and the body whom he had the honor to represent, would wish their fatherly counsel to this body so to be understood" to mean that American Methodists should free their slaves. The Rev. William Winans of Mississippi rejoined that the South "would not receive at the hands of British Methodists and Northern brethren, any help in the matter [of slavery]." The conference then passed a resolution paying "respectful deference" to their "elder brethren" but asserting in language reminiscent of the response of the Baptists to a British admonition the year before their belief that if the Wesleyans, with their "known prudence," had been well acquainted with the institution in America, . . . they would not have pressed the matter in such terms. Moreover, the conference by a vote of 140 to 14 agreed to condemn "modern abolitionism" and to censure not only Scott but also La Roy Sutherland, another preacher who had strongly supported the British messages.

The answer of the American Methodists to the British address of 1836 was prepared and forwarded to the Wesleyan Conference meeting in the United Kingdom the following July. But in August 1836, eighty-nine ministers from various New England and New York conferences rejected the reply of the American majority. Instead they accepted the British rebukes, as the Baptist dissidents in New England had done in previous years.

The majority of American Methodists, however, emphasized their rejection of the British messages by naming a vigorous critic of abolitionism, the Rev. Wilbur Fisk, as their delegate to the Wesleyan Conference in England that summer. Fisk assured the Britons that Garrisonian abolitionists in America were not men of the same caliber as Wilberforce, Thomas Clarkson, Granville Sharp, and other venerated leaders of the British cause. He felt sure "English gentlemen . . . [would] perceive the impropriety of direct interference with this question in America"; and he warned that agitation of the question was causing the American Methodist Church . . . to lose ground numerically. The reception of Fisk by the British brethren was far from cordial. Before the British Wesleyans assembled for their next conference in 1838, a convention of antislavery Methodists from all over the North met at Utica, New York; chose Orange Scott, censured by the General Conference in 1836, as special delegate to the British meeting; and sent the Rev. Luther Lee as delegate to the Canada Wesleyan Conference. The growing antislavery host among Northern Methodists was no longer willing to allow the majority coalition of Southerners and conservatives to determine representation of American Methodism at Wesleyan meetings in the British Empire.

Meantime, throughout the decade, antislavery messages from Britain continued to disturb American Methodists. When in 1837 the Georgia Conference passed a resolution denying that slavery was a moral evil, a position contrary to the Methodist Book of Discipline, British Methodists responded with an outraged denunciation. The *Christian Guardian,* organ of the Canada Conference, exploded with a tirade beginning with an invocation to the "Sainted spirit of the venerable Wesley!" In 1839 the British Conference met at Liverpool. Its address of the year reiterated the strictures against American slavery. . . . To the American quadrennial General Conference in 1840, held in New York City, the Britons again sent both an anti-slavery message and a delegate, the Rev. Robert Newton, who made the familiar exhortation to Americans to support abolitionism. The Americans responded in the familiar way. The message they adopted reassured Britons that the American church had not altered its Book of Discipline regarding slavery, but it insisted that emancipation was practically impossible in the Southern states and warned that abolitionist agitators were advocating defiance of the law of the land. "Methodism," the message continued, "has always been . . . eminently loyal and promotive of good order; and so we desire it may ever continue to be, both in Europe and in America."

Although a clear division of the Presbyterian Church along antislavery lines did not occur until shortly before the Civil War, the great schism of 1837–1838 resulting in the ejection of the New School was primarily a consequence of abolitionism, even though "the less embarrassing ground of heresy" was given for the split. So at least John Quincy Adams believed at the time, and he was a shrewd observer of national scene. A leading Presbyterian layman and abolitionist, James Gillespie Birney, also implied as much. In describing the division, he excoriated the Old School group, pointing out that its moderator, the Rev. William S. Plumer of Virginia, was the author of a somewhat sinister quip: "If abolitionists will set the country aflame, it is but fair that they should have the first warming at the fire." Such modern students of Presbyterian church history as E. A. Moore, Bruce Staiger, and W. W.

Sweet regard abolitionism as the crucial factor in the split.

British stimulus provided an important share of the abolitionist agitation that lay behind the schism, although the character of the stimulus was somewhat different from that affecting American Baptists and Methodists. Neither the Church of Scotland nor the Presbyterian churches in Ireland and England sent delegates to the General Assembly of the Presbyterian Church in the United States. The Congregational Union of England and Wales did, however, sponsor an official visitation by two of its ministers to further "friendly exchange and counsel and communion" between British Congregational and American Presbyterian as well as American Congregational bodies. The British emissaries, the Rev. Drs. Andrew Reed and James Matheson, toured the North in 1834; and "kind, brotherly exhortations" to oppose slavery comprised a large share of their message. A book recounting their mission created so hostile a stir in the United States that Harper and Brothers felt constrained to apologize for republishing it in America.

No official addresses from the national conventions of the British Presbyterians came to the sessions of the American General Assembly; but, during the two years preceding the schism, strong abolitionist messages from large Presbyterian groups in the United Kingdom were received by their American coreligionists. Twenty-two Scottish presbyteries and 350 congregations in 1836 adopted resolutions endorsing a long pamphlet entitled *Address on Negro Slavery, to the Christian Churches in the United States of America*. This address maintained that since its endorsers shared ancestry, doctrinal sentiments, and ecclesiastical polity with American Presbyterians, the reproof it conveyed was justifiable. . . . A similar address came in 1837 from the Presbyterians of Ulster, whence so many American Presbyterians had derived.

But probably the weightiest British contribution to the strife over slavery among American Presbyterians was made through the number of key figures in the revival of the American antislavery movement who either were British Presbyterian immigrants or received their initial antislavery impulse from British Presbyterians. One of the earliest examples of such a man was the Rev. George Bourne. He came to America near the close of the War of 1812 and became pastor of a congregation in Virginia, only to be relieved of his charge and accused of heresy by a council of the church in consequence of his *The Book and Slavery Irreconcilable,* published in 1816. Bourne moved North and became one of the most vitriolic of all abolitionists, fulminating against slaveholders and spicing his censures with tales of sex scandals that did not spare even Southern womanhood, treated as victim rather than culprit in most other antislavery propaganda. . . .

Several other Presbyterians who were spurred by British abolitionism were outstanding figures in the founding and early years of the American Anti-Slavery Society. Elected to the Society's first executive committee was the Rev. Abraham L. Cox. His brother, the Rev. Samuel H. Cox, was its first recording secretary. The Cox brothers were prominent American Presbyterian clergymen who had been converted at a church conference in Scotland in the summer of 1833 from support of the American Colonization Society to abolitionism by two eminent Scottish divines, the Rev. Drs. Thomas Ritchie and Thomas Chalmers. Samuel H. Cox

was one of the leaders of the New School faction in the schism of 1837. The first and perennial president of the American Anti-Slavery Society during its early years was the distinguished Presbyterian layman Arthur Tappan, wealthy New York merchant and unofficial "monarch" of the "benevolent empire." Tappan received tracts, books, and letters from British abolitionists during the final phases of the campaign for emancipation in the West Indies; and, as Gilbert H. Barnes has shown, it was through Theodore Weld, converted to abolitionism by the British Presbyterian Charles Stuart, that Arthur Tappan and his brother Lewis were persuaded to make antislavery one of the principal concerns of the "benevolent empire."

The devout Charles Stuart was perhaps responsible for bringing more American Presbyterians to antislavery convictions than any other Briton of that denomination. An enigmatic retired officer of the Royal Army, Stuart lived for a number of years in Canada and the United States before returning to Britain to play a leading role in the campaign for emancipation in the West Indies. He recrossed the Atlantic to America to join the antislavery crusade of the middle 1830's and spent the remainder of his life serving the cause of the Negro in the United States and the British Empire. He was a very important link between the antislavery movements of the two countries. Stuart reached New York in May 1834 fresh from his successes in England and just in time to address the first annual meeting of the American Anti-Slavery Society. He was immediately made a member of several committees and appointed agent—that is, a paid, traveling propagandist—for the Society. He was also commissioned to raise funds for the cause. From New York he hurried to Boston to address the New England Anti-Slavery Society, and then he commenced an abolitionist tour of New England, New York, and Ohio that lasted several years and resulted in the formation of innumerable local abolitionist groups and in increasing the membership of many already established. But Stuart's greatest influence in bringing Northerners and especially Northern Presbyterians to the support of the cause was attained not directly but through the career of his disciple, the tireless Presbyterian abolitionist, Theodore Weld. . . .

A few months after Charles Stuart began his American mission, the British Presbyterian abolitionist, George Thompson, arrived in New York to become a mainspring of the antislavery revival in the United States, as has already been seen in connection with Baptist and Methodist developments. Thompson, sent to America by several British abolitionist societies, was commissioned an agent of the American and New England Anti-Slavery societies after his arrival. A flamboyant orator, he conducted a boisterous fourteen-month crusade in the northeastern states, making some five hundred addresses, usually before large crowds, some friendly, others hostile. He was often jeered and threatened, and sometimes mobbed. He was denounced as a "fanatic" and "foreign incendiary" in much of the American press, in state legislatures, and in Congress, and even received adverse notice from President Jackson in a state of the Union message. By November 1835, when Thompson appeared a likely candidate for martyrdom, he left Boston suddenly and covertly for home. The antislavery societies, however, believed that the very glare of his publicity had been favorable to their cause,

and he was credited with partial and in some cases entire responsibility for the establishment of some three hundred new local auxiliaries to the national organization. . . .

Although in view of their past antislavery zeal American Quakers would not be expected to require any British stimulus in the 1830's, the fact is that when the American Anti-Slavery Society was founded in 1833, most leading Quakers remained aloof, and the Friends' coolness toward the new movement increased as the decade advanced. This situation puzzled and alarmed those Quakers from the older abolitionist school who did join the new movement, such as Isaac T. Hopper and Arnold Buffum. Some of them notified the British Quakers in 1834. The Meeting for Sufferings of London Yearly Meeting[2] responded almost at once by dispatching an epistle to every orthodox meeting in the United States, asking them to stand firmly on the law of Christ in asserting the rights of all Negroes not only to freedom but also to full religious and political equality. The message included the anticolonization statement that enjoyment of these rights should be "in the place where Providence has given them birth." This letter, quoted in the *American Anti-Slavery Reporter,* brought replies from almost every orthodox Quaker body in the country. Most of the responses protesting, as Methodist and Baptists had done, that the Britons were not aware of the complexity of the American problem, showed a reluctance to take the bold steps recommended by the London Friends. Some of

[2] That is, the presidium or permanent committee of the most influential Quaker body in the world. The quaint term Meeting for Sufferings derives from the days of Quaker persecution when the main business of such committees was to aid the victims.

them pointed out that Quakers, in their religious compact, already belonged to an abolition society.

The reluctance of American Friends to join the new antislavery societies was partly due to fears that the new agitation would compromise some of their other beliefs, such as nonviolence and other special aspects of their religious profession. William Bassett, a Massachusetts Friend who was also a Garrisonian abolitionist, wrote a long bitter letter to Elizabeth Pease, a British Quaker and philanthropist, complaining of the excuses American Quakers were given for avoiding abolitionists. Many Quakers, Bassett said, objected that the "premeditated preaching of abolitionists was inconsistent with the view of Friends on the immediate influence of the spirit." Paid antislavery agents they considered as bad as a hireling ministry, and they argued that Quakers were not supposed to mingle with members of other denominations in an enterprise which partook so much of a religious character. Bassett himself rejected all these excuses. The real reason for their reluctance, he maintained, was that the affluent and respectable American Friends shrank from association with the "obscure, despised, reviled, calumniated, abused, mobbed" abolitionists. Bassett concluded by sadly observing that the American Quaker endangered his reputation if he embraced abolitionism, while the English Quaker ruined his reputation if he did *not* embrace the cause.

British Quakers responded vigorously to such complaints. Influential leaders of the London and Birmingham meetings, like Joseph John Gurney and Joseph Sturge, who stopped off in the United States from trips to the West Indies to see how emancipation was working there, implored American Quakers to regain the antislavery energy of their fathers. Sturge held conferences with the Tappan brothers and other officials of the American Anti-Slavery Society in New York and planned an extended abolitionist tour of the country which he later made in the company of the poet John Greenleaf Whittier in 1841. Meanwhile, more messages were sent across the ocean from various British meetings, and the British reproofs were utilized in Quaker abolitionist tracts published in America. One such pamphlet paraphrased Job, "put our souls in their souls' stead," to illustrate the empathy for bondmen that always marked the finest Quaker antislavery testimony. The tension between conservative and abolitionist Friends, a tension significantly increased by recurrent British pressure, continued to grow throughout the decade.

During the 1840's the application of British antislavery energy to the American slavery problem persisted, but in a somewhat modified form from what it had been in the 1830's. The British and Foreign Anti-Slavery Society—a consolidation of many evangelical groups that still survived from the campaigns against bondage in the Empire—largely replaced the particular denominations in the task of stimulating attacks upon slavery under other flags. The new comprehensive organization sent across the Atlantic a stream of religious abolitionist tracts, and several of its founders or officers came to the United States and addressed both denominational and nondenominational antislavery meetings. In 1840 and 1843, the British and Foreign Anti-Slavery Society was host to world antislavery conventions in London. Both conventions passed resolutions requesting churches to withhold communion from slaveholders. Thousands of copies of the resolutions were distributed to American churches, and American abolitionists reported to their British coadjutors that many Northern congregations were acting in accordance with them. Conservatives, on the other hand, responded that the "church of Christ has no authority to make terms of communion which the apostles of Christ did not make." Tension within the churches continued to bear signs of British imposed stress.

Perhaps for this very reason, British antislavery Christians showed in many respects more restraint in pressing the cause upon Americans in the 1840's than they had in the 1830's. They sent no representatives to the stormy sessions which produced the disruptions of the great Baptist and Methodist denominations. Nor did they dispatch the familiar hortatory letters to these critical meetings. Probably they realized that at such crucial junctures, where Americans' emotions were already so strained, any further direct foreign interference within the denominations might endanger the cause.

Certainly many Americans of that day resented foreign criticism of slavery just as they do criticism of its sequel, racial discrimination, today. But the very bitterness of their resentment indicated a profound anxiety about foreign opinion. This anxiety was especially acute in the evangelical Protestant churches, and the churches were particularly sensitive to the judgment of their British counterparts, with whom they shared "ancestry, doctrinal sentiments, and ecclesiastical polity."

It is strange that historians have so largely ignored this sensitivity of American Protestants to British opinion in the matter of slavery and have failed in the main to mark its importance in the developments leading up both to the disruption of the largest denominations and to increased dissension in others, which Calhoun found so ominous. Contemporaries were keenly alert to the significance of the British pressures. Once the abolitionists had given up hope of converting the South, they worked to place the slaveholding area in a kind of moral isolation. Their estimate of the value of British support in this project was revealed in 1837 by the highest official in their movement, Arthur Tappan, president of the American Anti-Slavery Society. Writing to George Thompson, Tappan insisted that the countless messages from British churches had "greatly aided us in effecting that reformation of public opinion here which it is our object to effect" and that it had "contributed largely to bring back our Northern churches from the support of slavery." Keep helping us, Tappan asked, impose upon the South the "moral embargo of the civilized world."

Although Harwood does not assert that British influence was paramount in American antislavery affairs, his views, in combination with those of Barnes and Thistlethwaite, add weight to the idea that British influence permeated all aspects of the American movement. DAVID BRION DAVIS (1927–   ), professor of American history at Cornell University, takes exception to this point of view. Rejecting Barnes's and Thistlethwaite's conclusion that immediatism was a British doctrine adopted by the American Anti-Slavery Society to buttress its position, Davis maintains that the idea was a product of American as well as British antislavery thought and experience.*

Immediatism: A Product of American and British Antislavery Thought

In the history of reform few slogans have brought forth such confusion as "immediate emancipation." To the general public in the 1830's the phrase meant simply the abolition of Negro slavery without delay or preparation. But the word "immediate" may denote something other than a closeness of time; to many abolitionists it signified a rejection of intermediate agencies or conditions, a directness or forthrightness in action or decision. In this sense immediatism suggested a repudiation of the various media, such as colonization or apprenticeship, that had been advocated as remedies for the evils of slavery. To some reformers the phrase seemed mainly to imply a direct, intuitive consciousness of the sinfulness of slavery, and a sincere personal commitment to work for its abolition.[1] In this

[1] This was essentially the doctrine of the American Anti-Slavery Society in the 1830's. According to Gilbert H. Barnes, New York philanthropists borrowed the phrase from British abolitionists and interpreted it as meaning an honest and prompt beginning to gradual emancipation; but such jesuitical "gradualism in a British cloak" injured the cause, in Barnes's view, for many critics pointed out that the abolitionists must either be gradualists, in which case the slogan was meaningless, or favor instant and unconditional liberation of the slaves, which would be sheer madness. Yet the antislavery agents from Lane Seminary found in the

* From David Brion Davis, "The Emergence of Immediatism in British and American Antislavery Thought," *Mississippi Valley Historical Review*, XLIX (September, 1962), 209–230. Reprinted without most of the footnotes by permission of the Mississippi Valley Historical Association. Copyright © 1962 by the Mississippi Valley Historical Association.

subjective sense the word "immediate" was charged with religious overtones and referred more to the moral disposition of the reformer than to a particular plan for emancipation. Thus some reformers confused immediate abolition with an immediate personal decision to abstain from consuming slave-grown produce; and a man might be considered an immediatist if he were genuinely convinced that slavery should be abolished absolutely and without compromise, though not necessarily without honest preparation. Such a range of meanings led unavoidably to misunderstanding, and the antislavery cause may have suffered from so ambiguous a slogan. The ambiguity, however, was something more than semantic confusion or the unfortunate result of a misleading watchword. The doctrine of immediacy, in the form it took in the 1830's, was at once a logical culmination of the antislavery movement and a token of a major shift in intellectual history.

A belief in the slave's right to immediate freedom was at least implicit in much of the antislavery writing of the eighteenth century. . . . Several of the *philosophes* held that since masters relied on physical force to impose their illegal demands, slave revolts would be just; Louis de Jaucourt went so far as to argue that slaves, never having lost their inherent liberty, should be immediately declared free. Anthony Benezet advanced a similar argument, asking what course

a man should follow if he discovered that an inherited estate was really the property of another: "Would you not give it up immediately to the lawful owner? The voice of all mankind would mark him for a villain, who would refuse to comply with this demand of justice. And is not keeping a slave after you are convinced of the unlawfulness of it—a crime of the same nature?"

In England, Granville Sharp denounced slavery as a flagrant violation of the common law, the law of reason, and the law of God. After exhorting Lord North to do something about the plight of the slaves, he warned: "I say immediate redress, because, *to be in power,* and to neglect . . . even a day in endeavouring to put a stop to such monstrous injustice and abandoned wickedness, must necessarily endanger a man's *eternal* welfare, be he ever so great in *temporal* dignity or office." Sharp, who argued that "No Legislature on Earth . . . can alter the Nature of Things, or make that to be lawful, which is contrary to the Law of God," secured a judicial decision outlawing slavery in England. Americans like James Otis, Nathaniel Appleton, and Isaac Skillman took a similarly uncompromising stand before the Revolution; by the 1780's the doctrine of natural rights had made the illegality of slavery an established fact in Vermont and Massachusetts.

But the natural rights philosophy was not the only source of immediatism. Officially, the Society of Friends showed extreme caution in encouraging emancipation, but from the time of George Keith a latent impulse of moral perfectionism rose to the surface in the radical testimony of individual Quakers, who judged slavery in the uncompromising light of the Golden Rule. For re-

---

doctrine a way of emphasizing the sin of slavery and making their cause "identical with religion.". . . While Barnes shows that Americans were mainly preoccupied with the sin of slavery, he tends to overemphasize the British origins of immediatism and ignores the historical development of the doctrine in both countries. This criticism also applies to Stanley M. Elkins, *Slavery: A Problem in American Institutional and Intellectual Life* (Chicago, 1959).

formers, slavery was not a social or economic institution, but rather an embodiment of worldly sin that corrupted the souls of both master and slave; . . .

Immediatism, in the sense of an immediate consciousness of the guilt of slaveholding and an ardent desire to escape moral contamination, is similarly evident in the writings of men who differed widely in their views of religion and political economy. John Wesley's combined attack on the opposite poles of Calvinism and natural religion could also be directed against slavery, which some defended by arguments similar to those that justified seeming injustice or worldly evils as part of God's master plan or nature's economy. In 1784 Wesley's antislavery beliefs were developed into a kind of immediatism in the rules of American Methodists: "We ... think it our most bounden duty to take immediately some effectual method to extripate this abomination from among us." A related source of immediatism can be traced in the development of the romantic sensibility and the cult of the "man of feeling," which merged with Rousseau and the French Enlightenment in the writings of such men as Thomas Day and William Fox.

In the light of this evidence we may well ask why immediatism appeared so new and dangerously radical in the 1830's. The later abolitionists charged that slavery was a sin against God and a crime against nature; they demanded an immediate beginning of direct action that would eventuate in general emancipation. Yet all of this had been said at least a half-century before, and we might conclude that immediatism was merely a recurring element in antislavery history.

But if immediatism was at least latent in early antislavery thought, the dominant frame of mind of the eighteenth century was overwhelmingly disposed to gradualism. Gradualism, in the sense of a reliance on indirect and slow-working means to achieve a desired social objective, was the logical consequence of fundamental attitudes toward progress, natural law, property, and individual rights.

We cannot understand the force of gradualism in antislavery thought unless we abandon the conventional distinction between Enlightenment liberalism and evangelical reaction. It is significant that British opponents of abolition made little use of religion, appealing instead to the need for calm rationality and an expedient regard for the national interest. Quoting Hume, Lord Kames, and even Montesquieu to support their moral relativism, they showed that principles of the Enlightenment could be easily turned to the defense of slavery. A belief in progress and natural rights might lead, of course, to antislavery convictions; but if history seemed to be on the side of liberty, slavery had attained a certain prescriptive sanction as a nearly univeral expression of human nature. Men who had acquired an increasing respect for property and for the intricate workings of natural and social laws could not view as an unmitigated evil an institution that had developed through the centuries.

Though evangelicals attacked natural religion and an acceptance of the world as a divinely contrived mechanism in which evils like slavery served a legitimate function, they nevertheless absorbed many of the assumptions of conservative rationalists and tended to express a middle-class fear of sudden social change. Despite the sharp differences between evangelicals and rationalists, they shared confidence, for the most part, in the slow unfolding of a divine or natural plan of historical progress. The mild and almost imperceptible diffusion of reason, benevolence, or Christianity had made slavery—a vestige of barbarism —anachronistic. But while eighteenth-century abolitionists might delight in furthering God's or nature's plan for earthly salvation, they tended to assume a detached, contemplative view of history, and showed considerable fear of sudden changes or precipitous action that might break the delicate balance of natural and historical forces.

There was therefore a wide gap between the abstract proposition that slavery was wrong, or even criminal, and the cautious formulation of antislavery policy. It was an uncomfortable fact that slavery and the slave trade were tied closely to the rights of private property, the political freedom of colonies and states, and the economic rewards of international competition. Yet from the 1790's to the 1820's British and American reformers were confident that they understood the basic principles of society and could thus work toward the desired goal indirectly and without infringing on legitimate rights or interests. . . . The British reformers focused their attention on the slave trade, assuming that if the supply of African Negroes were shut off planters would be forced to take better care of their existing slaves and would ultimately discover that free labor was more profitable. In America, reform energies were increasingly directed toward removing the free Negroes, who were thought to be the principal barrier to voluntary manumission. Both schemes were attempts at rather complex social engineering, and in both instances the desired reform was to come from the slaveowners themselves. Antislavery theorists assumed that they could predict the cumulative effects and consequences of their limited programs, and since they never doubted the goodness or effectiveness of natural laws, they sought only to set in motion a chain of forces that would lead irresistibly to freedom.

This gradualist mentality dominated antislavery thought from the late eighteenth century to the 1820's. Though French thinkers had been among the first to denounce slavery as a crime, the emancipation scheme which they pioneered was one of slow transformation of the slave into a free laborer. Even the *Amis des Noirs* feared immediate emancipation; and the French decree abolishing slavery in 1794, which was the result of political and military crisis in the West Indies, seemed to verify the ominous warnings of gradualists in all countries. The years of bloodshed and anarchy in Haiti became an international symbol for the dangers of reckless and unplanned emancipation.

British abolitionists were particularly cautious in defining their objectives and moving indirectly, one step at a time. When outlawing the slave trade did not have the desired effect on colonial slavery, they then sought to bring the institution within the regulatory powers of the central government by limiting the extension of slavery in newly acquired islands and by using the crown colonies as models for gradual melioration; and when these efforts failed they urged a general registration of slaves, which would not only interpose imperial authority in the colonies but provide a mechanism for protecting the Negroes' rights. By 1822 these methods had proved inadequate and the British reformers began agitating for direct parliamentary intervention. Even then, however, and for the following eight years, British anti-slavery leaders limited their aims to melioration and emancipation by slow degrees.

Between British and American anti-slavery men there was a bond of understanding and a common interest in suppressing the international slave trade and finding a home in Haiti or western Africa for free Negroes. But in America the antislavery movement was given a distinctive color by the discouraging obstacles that stood in the way of even gradual emancipation. While states like New York and Pennsylvania provided tangible examples of gradual manumission, they also showed the harsh and ugly consequences of racial prejudice. Americans, far more than the British, were concerned with the problem of the emancipated slave. Even some of the most radical and outspoken abolitionists were convinced that colonization was the inescapable prerequisite to reform. Others stressed the importance of education and moral training as the first steps toward eventual freedom.

In America the gradualist frame of mind was also related to the weakness and limitations of political institutions. British abolitionists could work to enlist the unlimited power of a central Parliament against colonies that were suffering acute economic decline. But slavery in America was not only expanding but was protected by a sectional balance of power embodied in nearly every national institution. A brooding fear of disunion and anarchy damped down the aspirations of most American abolitionists and turned energies to such local questions as the education and legal protection of individual Negroes. Antislavery societies might call for the government to outlaw slavery in the District of Columbia or even to abolish the interstate slave trade,

but in the end they had to rely on public opinion and individual conscience in the slave states. While British abolitionists moved with the circumspection of conservative pragmatists, their American counterparts acted with the caution of men surrounded by high explosives. . . .

But if British and American abolitionists were gradualist in their policies and expectations, they did not necessarily regard slavery as simply one of many social evils that should be mitigated and eventually destroyed. The policy of gradualism was related to certain eighteenth-century assumptions about historical progress, the nature of man, and the principles of social change; but we have also noted a subjective, moral aspect to antislavery thought that was often revealed as an immediate consciousness of guilt and a fear of divine punishment. During the British slave trade controversy of the 1790's the entire system of slavery and slave trade became identified with sin, and reform with true virtue. Though antislavery leaders adopted the gradualist policy of choosing the slave trade as their primary target, they bitterly fought every attempt to meliorate or gradually destroy the African trade. It was the determined opponents of the slave trade who first gave popular currency to the slogan, "immediate abolition," which became in the early 1790's a badge of moral sincerity. When uncompromising hostility to the slave trade became a sign of personal virtue and practical Christianity, the rhetoric of statesmen acquired the strident, indignant tone that we associate with later American abolitionists. . . . "How shall we hope," asked William Pitt, "to obtain, if it is possible, forgiveness from Heaven for those enormous evils we have committed, if we refuse to make use of those means . . . for wiping away the guilt and shame with which we are now covered?"

This sense of moral urgency and fear of divine retribution persisted in British antislavery thought and was held in check only by a faith in the certain and predictable consequences of indirect action. Whenever the faith was shaken by unforeseen obstacles or a sense of crisis, there were voices that condemned gradualism as a compromise with sin. Granville Sharp, who interpreted hurricanes in the West Indies as supernatural agencies "to blast the *enemies* of *law* and *righteousness*," called in 1806 for direct emancipation by act of Parliament, and warned that continued toleration of slavery in the colonies "must finally draw down the Divine vengeance upon our state and nation!" When William Allen, Zachary Macaulay, and James Cropper became disillusioned over the failure to secure an effective registration scheme and international suppression of the slave trade, they pressed for direct though gradual emancipation by the British government. The British Anti-Slavery Society remained officially gradualist until 1831, but individual abolitionists, particularly in the provinces, became increasingly impatient over the diffidence of the government and the intransigence of colonial legislatures.[2] From 1823 to 1832 the British Caribbean planters violently attacked the government's efforts to meliorate slavery. They not only devised schemes to nullify effective reform but threatened to secede from the empire and seek protection from the United States. Though the evils of West Indian slavery were probably mitigated in the 1820's, the planters' resistance convinced many abolitionists that gradual improvement was impossible.

The most eloquent early plea for immediate emancipation was made in 1824 by a Quaker named Elizabeth Heyrick, who looked to the women of Great Britain as a source of invicible moral power, and who preached a massive consumers' crusade against West Indian produce. The central theme in Mrs. Heyrick's pamphlet, *Immediate, Not Gradual Abolition,* was the supremacy of individual conscience over social and political institutions. . . . Like the later American immediatists, she excoriated gradualism as a satanic plot to induce gradual indifference. . . . For Mrs. Heyrick the issue was simple and clearcut: sin and vice should be immediately exterminated by individual action in accordance with conscience and the will of God.

In 1824 such views were too strong for British antislavery leaders, who still looked to direct government action modeled on the precedent of the Canning Resolutions, which had proposed measures for ameliorating the condition of West Indian slaves as a step toward ultimate emancipation. Abolitionists in Parliament continued to shape their strategy in the light of political realities, but by 1830 several prominent reformers had adopted the uncompromising stand of Elizabeth Heyrick. The shift from gradualism to immediatism is most dramatically seen in James Stephen, who possessed a mind of great clarity and precision and who, having practiced law in the West Indies, had acquired direct experience with slavery as an institution. For a time Stephen adhered to the principle of gradualism. . . . By 1830, how-

---

[2] In the 1830's American abolitionists claimed that the British Anti-Slavery Society had adopted the principle of immediatism in 1826, and later historians have repeated the same error. It was only in 1831 and 1832 that immediatism gained widespread support, and even then the more conservative leaders looked to the government for an effective but gradual working plan.

ever, he was convinced that debate over alternative plans merely inhibited action and obscured what was essentially a question of principle and simple moral duty. . . . Lashing out at the moral lethargy of the government, he denounced the principle of compensation to slaveowners and rejected all specific gradualist measures such as the liberation of Negro women or the emancipation of infants born after a certain date. Stephen's immediatism was based ultimately on a fear of divine vengeance and an overwhelming sense of national guilt. . . .

On October 19, 1830, the Reverend Andrew Thomson, of St. George's Church in Edinburgh, delivered a fire-and-brimstone speech that provided an ideology for George Thompson and the later Agency Committee. Beginning with the premise that slavery is a crime and sin, Thomson dismissed all consideration of economic and political questions. When the issue was reduced to what individual men should do as mortal and accountable beings, there was no possibility of compromise or even controversy. The British public should "compel" Parliament to order total and immediate emancipation. With Calvinistic intensity he exhorted the public to cut down and burn the "pestiferous tree, root and branch: "You must annihilate it, — annihilate it now, — and annihilate it forever." Since Thomson considered every hour that men were kept in bondage a repetition of the original sin of man-stealing, he did not shrink from violence: "If there must be violence, . . . let it come and rage its little hour, since it is to be succeeded by lasting freedom, and prosperity, and happiness."

Taking its cue from men like Stephen, Thomson, and Joseph Sturge, the Anti-Slavery Society reorganized itself for more effective action and focused its energies on raising petitions and arousing public feeling against slavery. While Thomas Fowell Buxton sought to make the fullest use of public opinion to support his campaign in Parliament, he found himself under mounting pressure from abolitionists who refused to defer to his judgment. People's principles, he told his daughter, were the greatest nuisance in life. When the government finally revealed its plan for gradual and compensated emancipation, the Anti-Slavery Society committed itself to vigorous and aggressive opposition. But once the law had been passed, the antislavery leaders concluded that they had done as well as possible and that their defeat had actually been a spectacular victory. They had achieved their primary object, which was to induce the people to support a tangible act that could be interpreted as purging the nation of collective guilt and proving the moral power of individual conscience.

In America the developing pattern was somewhat similar. Despite the conservatism of most antislavery societies, a number of radical abolitionists branded slaveholding as a heinous sin, which, if not immediately abandoned, would bring down the wrath of the Lord. A few early reformers like Theodore Dwight, David Rice, Charles Osborn, and John Rankin, were well in advance of British antislavery writers in their sense of moral urgency and their mistrust of gradualist programs. As early as 1808, David Barrow, although he denied favoring immediate abolition, anticipated the later doctrine of the American Anti-Slavery Society by refusing to recognize the lawfulness of slavery or the justice of compensation. Holding that slavery was the crying sin of America, he urged a prompt beginning of manumission in order to avert the retribution of God. Three years ear-

lier Thomas Branagan, who opposed "in-
stantaneous emancipation" if the freed
Negroes were to remain within the
United States, contended that his plan
for colonization in the West would bring
a speedy end to slavery and avert the
divine judgment of an apocalyptic racial
war. In 1817 John Kenrick showed that
colonization could be combined with a
kind of immediatism, for though he proposed settlement of free Negroes in the
West, he went so far as to suggest that
the powers of the central government
should be enlarged, if necessary, in order
to abolish slavery. "If slavery is 'a violation of the divine laws,'" Kenrick asked,
"is it not absurd to talk about a gradual
emancipation? We might as well talk of
gradually leaving off piracy — murder —
adultery, or drunkenness."

The religious character of this radical
abolitionism can best be seen in the writings of George Bourne, an English immigrant who was to have a deep influence on William Lloyd Garrison. In
1815 Bourne condemned professed Christians who upheld the crime of slavery.
"The system is so entirely corrupt," he
wrote, "that it admits of no cure, but
by a total and immediate, abolition. For
a gradual emancipation is a virtual recognition of the right, and establishes
the rectitude of the practice." But while
Bourne associated slavery with the very
essence of human sin, his main concern
was not the plight of Negroes but the
corruption of the Christian church. . . .
Thus for Bourne "immediatism" meant
an immediate recognition of the sin of
slavery and an immediate decision on the
part of Christians to purge their churches
of all contamination. He was far more
interested in the purification of religion
than in slavery as an institution.

In 1825 the Boston *Recorder and Tele-
graph* published a long correspondence
that further clarifies the origins of immediatism. After arguing that slavery
was unlawful and suggesting that slaves
might have a right to revolt, "Vigornius"
[Samuel M. Worcester] asserted that *the
slave-holding system must be abolished;*
and in order to the accomplishment of
this end, immediate, determined measures must be adopted for the ultimate
emancipation of every slave within our
territories." This was the position of the
later Kentucky and New York abolitionists, but Vigornius combined it with
strong faith in the American Colonization Society. He was bitterly attacked
by "A Carolinian," who accused him of
believing in "an entire and immediate
abolition of slavery." "Philo," the next
contributor, said he opposed immediate
emancipation on grounds of expediency,
but recognized the right of slaves to immediate freedom; he advocated, therefore, "immediate and powerful remedies," since "We are convinced, and if
our Southern brethren are not convinced,
we wish to convince them, and think
with a little discussion we could convince
them, that to postpone these prospective
measures a day, is a great crime . . . and
moreover, we wish to state directly, that
this postponement is that, in which we
consider the guilt of slavery, so far as
the present proprietors are concerned, to
consist."

A Southerner, who called himself
"Hieronymus," defended Vigornius and
tried to avoid the ambiguities that were
later to cloud discussions of immediate
abolition. Vigornius, he wrote,

pleads, it is true, for *speedy* emancipation,
and immediate preparatory steps. But immediate and speedy are not synonimous [sic]
expressions. One is an absolute, the other a
relative or comparative term. An event may
in one view of it be regarded as very speedy,
which in another might be pronounced very

gradual. If slavery should be entirely abolished from the United States in 30, 40, or even 50 years, many . . . will readily admit, that it would be a speedy abolition; while every one must perceive, that it would be far, very far, from an immediate abolition. In a certain sense abolition may be immediate; in another, speedy; and in both, practicable and safe. . . .

Hieronymus, who had read and been impressed by Elizabeth Heyrick's pamphlet, agreed with Vigornius that colonization was the only practicable solution to the nation's most critical problem.

These ardent colonizationists believed that slavery was a sin that would increase in magnitude and danger unless effective measures were adopted without delay. Yet by 1821 Benjamin Lundy and other abolitionists had come to the opinion that the American Colonization Society was founded on racial prejudice and offered no real promise of undermining slavery. Lundy thought that slavery could not be eradicated until his fellow Americans in both North and South were willing to accept the free Negro as an equal citizen. But in the meantime the institution was expanding into the Southwest and even threatening to spread to such states as Illinois. In the face of such an imposing problem, Lundy called for the swift and decisive use of political power by a convention of representatives from the various states, who might devise and implement a comprehensive plan for emancipation.[3]

The American antislavery organizations absorbed some of this sense of urgency and mistrust of palliatives. The Pennsylvania Society for the Abolition of

Slavery was cautious in its approach to the national problem, but in 1819 it approved a declaration that "the practice of holding and selling human beings as property . . . ought to be *immediately* abandoned." In 1825 the Acting Committee of the American Convention for Promoting the Abolition of Slavery advocated the "speedy and entire" emancipation of slaves, a phrase later used by the British Society. The convention showed little confidence in any of the specific proposals for gradual abolition but at the same time rejected direct emancipation by act of Congress as an impossibility. Alert always to the need for conciliating the South and remaining within the prescribed bounds of the Constitution, the Convention considered every conceivable plan in a rationalistic and eclectic spirit. In the South, however, there was an increasing tendency to see the most conservative antislavery proposals as immediatism in disguise. By 1829 the gradualist approach of the American Convention had reached a dead end.

It is a striking coincidence that both the British and American antislavery movements had come to a crucial turning point by 1830. In both countries the decline of faith in gradualism had been marked in the mid-1820's by enthusiasm for a boycot of slave produce, a movement which promised to give a cutting edge to the moral testimony of individuals. In both countries the truculence and stubborn opposition of slaveholders to even gradualist reforms brought a sense of despair and indignation to the antislavery public. To some degree immediatism was the creation of the British and American slaveholders themselves. By accusing the most moderate critics of radical designs and by blocking the path to many attempted reforms they helped

[3] Lundy favored colonization at public expense of Negroes wishing to leave the country, but he also called on the North to receive emancipated slaves without restriction, and exhorted the South to repeal laws discriminating against free Negroes.

to discredit the gradualist mentality that had balanced and compromised a subjective conviction that slavery was sin. The sense of crisis between 1829 and 1831 was also accentuated by an increasing militancy of Negroes, both slave and free. In 1829 David Walker hinted ominously of slave revenge; groups of free Negroes openly repudiated the colonization movement; and in 1831 bloody revolts erupted in Virginia and Jamaica. In that year a new generation of American reformers adopted the principle of immediatism, which had recently acquired the sanction of eminent British philanthropists. But while American abolitionists modeled their new societies and techniques on British examples, the principle of immediatism had had a long and parallel development in both countries.

In one sense immediatism was simply a shift in strategy brought on by the failure of less direct plans for abolition. Earlier plans and programs had evoked little popular excitement compared with parliamentary reform or Catholic emancipation in England, or with tariff or land policies in the United States. As a simple, emotional slogan, immediate abolition would at least arouse interest and perhaps appeal to the moral sense of the public. As a device for propaganda, it had the virtue of avoiding economic and social complexities and focusing attention on a clear issue of right and wrong. If the public could once be brought to the conviction that slavery was wrong and that something must be done about it at once, then governments would be forced to take care of the details.

But immediatism was something more than a shift in strategy. It represented a shift in total outlook from a detached, rationalistic perspective on human history and progress to a personal commitment to make no compromise with sin.

It marked a liberation for the reformer from the ideology of gradualism, from a toleration of evil within the social order, and from a deference to institutions that blocked the way to personal salvation. Acceptance of immediatism was the sign of an immediate transformation within the reformer himself; as such, it was seen as an expression of inner freedom, or moral sincerity and earnestness, and of victory over selfish and calculating expediency. If slaveholders received the doctrine with contempt and scathing abuse, the abolitionist was at least assured of his own freedom from guilt. He saw the emergence of immediatism as an upswelling of personal moral force which, with the aid of God, would triumph over all that was mean and selfish and worldly.

There are obvious links between immediate emancipation and a religious sense of immediate justification and presence of the divine spirit that can be traced through the early spiritual religions to the Quakers, Methodists, and evangelical revivals. The new abolitionism contained a similar pattern of intense personal anxiety, rapturous freedom, eagerness for sacrifice, and mistrust of legalism, institutions, and slow-working agencies for salvation. It was no accident that from the late seventeenth century the boldest assertions of antislavery sentiment had been made by men who were dissatisfied with the materialism and sluggish formality of institutionalized religion, and who searched for a fresh and assuring meaning of Christian doctrine in a changing world.[4] To the

---

[4] There is a clear relationship between antislavery and religious anxiety in the lives of many abolitionists. Obviously, most religious anxiety found other outlets than antislavery; but the writings of abolitionists in both Britain and America show that the cause satisfied religious yearnings that could not be fulfilled by the traditional institutions of the church.

extent that slavery became a concrete symbol of sin, and support of the antislavery cause a sign of Christian virtue, participation in the reform became a supplement or even alternative to traditional religion. As a kind of surrogate religion, antislavery had long shown tendencies that were pietistic, milennial, and anti-institutional. By the 1830's it had clearly marked affinities with the increasingly popular doctrines of free grace, immediate conversion, and personal holiness. According to Amos A. Phelps, for example, immediatism was synonymous with immediate repentance: "All that follows is the carrying out of the new principle of action, and is to emancipation just what sanctification is to conversion."

Immediate emancipation was also related to a changing view of history and human nature. Whereas the gradualist saw man as at least partially conditioned by historical and social forces, the immediatist saw him as essentially indeterminate and unconditioned. The gradualist, having faith in the certainty of economic and social laws, and fearing the dangers of a sudden collapse of social controls, was content to wait until a legal and rational system of external discipline replaced the arbitrary power of the slaveowner. The immediatist, on the other hand, put his faith in the innate moral capacities of the individual. He felt that unless stifling and coercive influences were swept away, there could be no development of the inner controls of conscience, emulation, and self-respect, on which a free and Christian society depended. His outlook was essentially romantic, for instead of cautiously manipulating the external forces of nature, he sought to create a new epoch of history by liberating the inner moral forces of human nature.[5]

It falls beyond the scope of the present essay to show how immediatism itself became institutionalized as a rigid test of faith, and how it served as a medium for attacking all rival institutions that limited individual freedom or defined standards of thought and conduct. It is enough to suggest that immediatism, while latent in early antislavery thought, was part of a larger reaction against a type of mind that tended to think of history in terms of linear time and logical categories, and that emphasized the importance of self-interest, expediency, moderation, and planning in accordance with economic and social laws. Immediatism shared with the romantic frame of mind a hostility to all dualisms of thought and feelings, and allegiance to both emotional sympathy and abstract principle, an assumption that mind can rise above self-interest, and a belief that ideas, when held with sufficient intensity, can be transformed into irresistible moral action. If immediate emancipation brought misunderstanding and violent hostility in regions that were charged with racial prejudice and fear of sectional conflict, it was nevertheless an appropriate doctrine for a romantic and evangelical age.

[5] ... Stanley Elkins correctly discerns the antiformal and anti-institutional character of immediatism (*Slavery*, 189–92), but he relates it to the fluid social structure in the United States; the same characteristics had been present in British and French antislavery literature from the eighteenth century, and their accentuation by the 1830's would seem to have been part of a major ideological development.

Historians are divided in evaluating the effects
of abolitionism on the sectional crisis of the 1840s
and 1850s. In this selection AVERY O. CRAVEN
(1889–   ), emeritus professor of American history
at the University of Chicago, asserts that the Civil War
was a "needless conflict" precipitated primarily
by fear, hatred, and hysteria aroused by the extreme
doctrines of Northern abolitionists.*

Irresponsible Fanatics

The abolition movement . . . was closely related in origins, leadership, and expression to the peace movement, the temperance crusade, the struggles for women's rights, prison and Sabbath reform, and the improvement of education. It was not unrelated to the efforts to establish communities where social-economic justice and high thinking might prevail. It was part of the drive to unseat aristocrats and re-establish American democracy according to the Declaration of Independence. It was a clear-cut effort to apply Christianity to the American social order.

The anti-slavery effort was at first merely one among many. It rose to dominance only gradually. Fortunate from the beginning in leadership, it was always more fortunate in appeal. Human slavery more obviously violated democratic institutions than any other evil of the day; it was close enough to irritate and to inflame sensitive minds, yet far enough removed that reformers need have few personal relations with those whose interests were affected. It rasped most severely upon the moral senses of a people whose ideas of sin were comprehended largely in terms of self-indulgence and whose religious doctrines laid emphasis on social usefulness as the proper manifestation of salvation. And, what was more important, slavery was now confined to a section whose economic interests, and hence political attitudes, con-

* Reprinted from *The Coming of the Civil War* by Avery O. Craven without footnotes by permission of The University of Chicago Press. Copyright 1942 by Charles Scribner's Sons; Second edition © by Avery Craven. Published 1957. Printed by The University of Chicago Press, Chicago, Ill., U.S.A. Pp. 134–150.

flicted sharply with those of the Northeast and upper Northwest.

Almost from the beginning of the new antislavery movement, two distinct centers of action appeared, each with its distinct and individual approach to the problem. One developed in the industrial areas of New England. Its most important spokesman was William Lloyd Garrison, founder and editor of a Boston abolition paper called the *Liberator*. Garrison at first accepted the old idea that slavery was an *evil* to be pointed out and gradually eradicated by those among whom it existed, but he shifted his position in the early 1830's and denounced slavery as a damning crime to be unremittingly assailed and immediately destroyed. The first issue of his paper announced a program from which he never deviated: "*. . . I do not wish to think or speak or write with moderation. I will not retreat a single inch, and I will be heard.*" The problem, as Garrison saw it, was one of abstract right and wrong. The Scriptures and the Declaration of Independence had already settled the issue. Slavery could have no legal status in a Christian democracy. If the Constitution recognized it, then the Constitution should be destroyed. Slaveholders were both sinners and criminals. They could lay no claim to immunity from any mode of attack.

The character of this movement and its leadership is strikingly revealed in an incident related by one of Garrison's traveling companions:

As we rode through the [Franconia] Notch after friends Beach and Rogers, we were alarmed at seeing smoke issue from their chaise-top, and we cried out to them that their chaise was afire! We were more than suspicious that it was something worse than that, and that the smoke came out of friend Rogers' mouth. And so it turned out. This was before we reached the Notch tavern. Alighting there to water our beasts, we gave him, all round a faithful admonition. For anti-slavery does not fail to spend its intervals of public service in mutual and searching correction of the faults of its friends. We gave it soundly to friend Rogers—that he, an abolitionist, on his way to an anti-slavery meeting, should desecrate his anti-slavery mouth . . . with a stupefying weed. We had halted at the Iron Works tavern to refresh our horses, and while they were eating walked to view the Furnace. As we crossed the little bridge, friend Rogers took out another cigar, as if to light it when we should reach the fire! "Is it any malady you have got, brother Rogers," said we to him, "that you smoke that thing, or is it habit and indulgence merely?" It is nothing but habit," said he gravely; "or I would say, it was nothing else," and he significantly cast the little roll over the railing into the Ammonoosuck.

"A Revolution!" exclaimed Garrison, "a glorious revolution without noise or smoke," and he swung his hat cheerily about his head. It was a pretty incident. . . . It was a vice abandoned, a self indulgence denied, and from principle. It was quietly and beautifully done. . . . Anti-slavery wants her mouths for other uses than to be flues for besotting tobacco-smoke. They may as well almost be rum-ducts as tobacco-funnels. . . . Abolitionists are generally as *crazy* in regard to rum and tobacco as in regard to slavery. Some of them refrain from eating flesh and drinking tea and coffee. Some of them are so bewildered that they want in the way of Christian retaliation . . . they are getting to be monomoniacs, as the Reverend Punchard called us, on *every* subject.

The extreme and impractical nature of the Garrison antislavery drive served to attract attention and arouse antagonism rather than to solve the problem. It did, however, show how profoundly the conditions of the time had stirred the reform spirit and how wide the door had

been opened to the professional reformers—men to whom the question was not
so much "how shall we abolish slavery,
as how shall we best discharge our duty
. . . to ourselves." Garrison may be taken
as typical of the group. His temperament
and experiences had combined to set him
in most relationships against the accepted
order of things. His life would probably
have been spent in protesting even if
slavery had never existed. From childhood he had waged a bitter fight *against*
obstacles and *for* a due recognition of his
abilities. A drunken father had abandoned the family to extreme poverty before William was three years old, and the
boy, denied all but the rudiments of an
education, had first been placed under
the care of Deacon Bartlett, and then
apprenticed for seven years to one Eph-
raim Allen to learn the printing trade.
His first venture after his apprenticeship
was over failed. His second gave him the
opportunity to strike back at an unfair
world. He became an editor of the *National Philanthropist,* a paper devoted
to the suppression of "intemperance and
its Kindred vices." This publication
served also as a medium through which
to attack lotteries, Sabbath-breaking, and
war. A new Garrison began to emerge.
His personality, given opportunity for
expression, asserted itself. Attending a
nominating caucus in Boston, he made
bold to speak, and, being resented as an
upstart, he replied to his critic in a letter
to the Boston *Courier*:

It is true my acquaintance in this city is
limited. . . . Let me assure him, however,
that if my life be spared, my name shall one
day be known to the world—at least to such
an extent that common inquiry shall be un-
necessary.

To another critic he reiterated this state-

ment, adding these significant words: "I
speak in the spirit of prophecy, not of
vainglory—with a strong pulse, a flashing
eye, and a glow of the heart. The task
may be yours to write my biography."

Anti-slavery efforts entered the Garrison program when Benjamin Lundy, the
pioneer abolitionist, invited him to help
edit the *Genius of Universal Emancipation* in Baltimore. Hostile treatment
there, climaxed by imprisonment for
libel, together with the influence of extreme British opinion, changed a moderate attitude which admitted "that immediate and complete emancipation is
not desirable . . . no rational man cher-
ishes so wild a vision," into the extreme
and uncompromising fanaticism expressed only two years later in the *Liberator*. From that time on Garrison was
bothered only by the fact that the English language was inadequate for the
expression of his violent opinions. Southerners in Congress were desperados.

We would sooner trust the honor of the
country . . . in the hands of the inmates of
our penitentiaries and prisons than in their
hands . . . they are the meanest of thieves
and the worst of robbers. . . . We do not
acknowledge them to be within the pale of
Christianity, or republicanism, or humanity!

Hatred of the South had supplanted love
for the Negro!

In such an approach as this, there
could be no delay, no moderation. Right
was right, and wrong was wrong. The
slaveholder could not be spared or given
time to learn the evil of his ways. Action
immediate and untempered was demanded. . . .

The second center of anti-slavery effort
was in upper New York and the farther
Northwest. Influences from this center
included in their sweep, however, much

of rural New England and the Middle States and the movement found liberal financial help in New York City. Benjamin Lundy and other Quaker leaders started the crusade, but it did not come to full and wide expression until Theodore Weld, already the ablest temperance orator in the Northwest, set about cultivating the great field prepared for social reform by the Finney revivals.

Weld was, like Garrison, unusual both in abilities and in personal characteristics. He was much given to "anti-meat, -butter, -tea, and -coffee, etc. -ism[s]." He indulged in excessive self-effacement and in extravagant confessions of selfishness, pride, impatience of contradition, personal recklessness, and "a bad, unlovely temper." . . .

He had the Puritan's love of enduring; the saint's "right" to intolerance. He was, in fact, always a revivalist—a man with a mission to perform in the great West—"the battlefield of the World."

The campaign which he launched was but an expansion of the benevolence crusade already a part of the Western revival effort. As W. C. Preston said: "Weld's agents made the anti-slavery cause 'identical with religion,' and urged men, by all they esteem[ed] holy, by all the high and existing obligations of duty to man and God . . . to join the pious work of purging the sin of slavery from the land." The movement, as it developed, was generally temperate in tone, and tended to function through the existing agencies of religion and politics. Lane Theological Seminary, founded in Cincinnati to train leaders in the Finney tradition, became the center from which Weld worked. Here, in a series of debates, he shaped the doctrine of gradual immediatism which by insisting that *gradual emancipation* begin *at once*,

saved the movement from Garrison's extremes; from here he went out to win a group of converts which included James G. Birney, Joshua Giddings, Edwin M. Stanton, Elizur Wright, and Beriah Green; and here he adapted the revival technique to the abolition crusade and prepared the way for his loyal band of Seventy to carry that crusade throughout the whole Northwest.

There was, however, another aspect to the movement in this region—a very hard-headed practical aspect. Its leaders believed in action as well as agitation. And action here meant political action. Western men had a way of viewing evil as something there ought to be a law against. They thought it was the business of government to secure morality as well as prosperity. They were even inclined to regard the absence of prosperity as the result of the existence of evil. Naturally, therefore, in spite of the revival-meeting procedure used to spread the gospel of abolition, action against slavery followed political precedent. This action began with petitions to Congress for such a practical end as the abolition of slavery in the District of Columbia. When Southern resentment of such a measure brought the adoption of gag rule methods, the contest was broadened into a fight on the floors of Congress for the constitutional rights of petition and free speech. This proved to be an excellent way to keep the slavery question before the public and to force slaveholders to reveal their undemocratic attitudes. Petitions arrived in such quantities as to clog the work of Congress. A Washington organization for agitation and lobbying became necessary. Weld himself went to Washington to advise with John Quincy Adams and his fellow workers. Slavery thus again entered national politics, this time by way of the Northwest. Antislavery politicians, such as Joshua Giddings and Salmon P. Chase of Ohio, quickly proved the value of the cause as a stepping-stone to public office.

James Birney took the next step. The indifference of old political parties to petitions and abolition demands gave rise to the belief that the slave interest controlled their programs. The conviction that the welfare of other sections was being neglected for the advancement of the South followed logically upon this premise. The slave power, said the abolitionists, had already destroyed the protective system "at the hazard, if not with the intention" of breaking up the manufacturing interests of the free states. The federal government had developed and protected markets for cotton "in all parts of the known world, while it studiously avoided doing anything to procure a market for the free products of the grain-growing Northwest." As a result wheat had been stacked seven successive years in the fields, and none sold. The United States had sent

six expensive embassies to make markets for tobacco. We had one embassy six years to get money for a few slaves wrecked on a British colony; but not one to find a market for the astonishing produce of the great Northwest. We've been thirty years toiling to keep a market for cotton; but not an hour for wheat. If our government was honest; if our statesmen had eyes, they would see that the most important benefit they could render this country would be to find a market for the produce of the Northwest. . . .

Anti-slavery must organize a political party.

The Liberty Party entered the national field in 1840 with James G. Birney as its candidate. It was a protest party. In his acceptance letter, Birney declared that the country was in the hands of the slave power—"the North . . . a conquered province." Its honor, its influence and the real prosperity of the nation had declined in proportion to Southern rule. Tariffs, beneficial to free labor, had been abandoned; monetary affairs had become deranged; commercial opportunities had been neglected. Abolitionists could vote for neither Van Buren nor Harrison.

Having issued this statement, the Liberty Party candidate set out for London to attend the General Anti-Slavery Convention of 1840. He carried with him to the English Anti-Corn Law League a mass of propaganda designed to aid in opening the English markets for the wheat crops of the Old Northwest. His general purpose was to secure the withdrawal of all British restrictions on American wheat and to encourage the growth in India of cotton for English factories. English commercial interests would thus be shifted from the South to the North and slavery in American cotton fields would be rendered unprofitable. Throughout the summer and fall, Birney waged his presidential campaign on British soil. Back home the dejected wheat farmers of the Northwest organized Anti-Corn Law Societies to help influence the course of English politics!

As economic rivalry between North and South increased, the antislavery movement gained strength and began to emerge as the dominant reform effort of the period. The motives underlying this development are partly revealed by a letter written by Joshua Leavitt to his friend Joshua Giddings in October, 1841. Leavitt spoke of Giddings' belief that the best policy for action was to aim "at specific points . . . which you deem beneficial to free labor or rather to the North, as a bank, tariff, etc." and then declared that his own purpose was to make opposition to slavery the *leading object* of public policy. "We must have a leading object," he continued,

in which we can all harmonize, and to which we shall agree to defer all other favorite objects. It is vain to think of harmonizing the North in favor of a restrictive policy or an artificial credit system. . . . There is no object but slavery that can serve our turn . . . it is the greatest of evils and the prime cause of other evils. . . .

With the new growth and new importance of the movement, the technique of its propaganda also reached new efficiency. Never before or since has a cause been urged upon the American people with such consummate skill and such lasting effects. Every agency possible in that day was brought into use; even now the predominating opinions of most of the American people regarding the antebellum South and its ways are the product of that campaign of education.

Indoctrination began with the child's A B C's which were learned from booklets containing verses like the following:

A is an Abolitionist
A man who wants to free
The wretched slave, and give to all
An equal liberty.

B is a Brother with a skin
Of somewhat darker hue,
But in our Heavenly Father's sight,
He is as dear as you.

C is the Cotton field, to which
This injured brother's driven,
When, as the white man's *slave,* he toils
From early morn till even.

D is the Driver, cold and stern,
Who follows, whip in hand,
To punish those who dare to rest,
Or disobey command.

. . . .

I is the Infant, from the arms
Of its fond mother torn,
And at a public auction sold
With horses, cows, and corn.

. . . .

Q is the Quarter, where the slave
On coarsest food is fed
And where, with toil and sorrow worn
He seeks his wretched bed.

. . . .

W is the Whipping post,
To which the slave is bound,
While on his naked back, the lash
Makes many a bleeding wound.

. . . .

Z is a Zealous man, sincere,
Faithful, and just, and true;
An earnest pleader for the slave—
Will you not be so too?

. . . For adults the appeal was widened. No approach was neglected. Hymn books offered abolition songs set to familiar tunes. To the strains of "Old Hundred" eager voices invited "ye Yeomen brave" to rescue "the bleeding slave," or, to the "Missionary Hymn," asked them to consider

The frantic mother
Lamenting for her child,
Till falling lashes smother
Her cries of anguish wild!

Almanacs, carrying the usual information about weather and crops, filled their other pages with abolition propaganda. In one of these, readers found the story of Liburn Lewis, who, for a trifling offense, bound his slave, George, to a meat block and then, while all the other slaves looked on, proceeded slowly to chop him to pieces with a broad ax, and to cast the parts into a fire. Local, state, and national societies were organized for more efficient action in petitioning, presenting public speakers, distributing tracts, and publishing anti-slavery periodicals. The American Anti-Slavery Society "in the year 1837–38, published 7,877 bound volumes, 47,256 tracts and pamphlets, 4,100 circulars, and 10,490 prints. Its quarterly *Anti-Slavery Magazine* had an annual circulation of 9,000; the *Slave Friend,* for children, had 131,050; the monthly *Human Rights,* 189,400, and the weekly *Emancipator,* 217,000." From 1854 to 1858 it spent $3281 on a series of tracts discussing every phase of slavery, under such suggestive titles as "Disunion, our Wisdom and our Duty," "Relations of Anti-Slavery to Religion," and "To Mothers in the Free States." Its "several corps of lecturers of the highest ability and worth . . . occupied the field" every year in different states. Its Annual Reports, with their stories of atrocities and their biased discussion of issues, constituted a veritable arsenal from which weapons of attack could be drawn. Like other antislavery societies, it maintained an official organ, issued weekly, and held its regular conventions for the generation of greater force.

Where argument and appeal to reason failed, the abolitionists tried entertainment and appeal to emotion. *Uncle Tom's Cabin* was written because its author, "as a woman, as a mother," was "oppressed and broken hearted, with the sorrows & injustice" seen, and "because as a Christian" she "felt the dishonor to Christianity—because as a lover of [her] country, [she] trembled at the coming day of wrath." It became a best seller in the most complete sense. Only the Bible exceeded it in numbers sold and in the thoroughness with which it was read in England and America. . . .

Reformed slaveholders and escaped slaves were especially valuable in the crusade. Under the warming influence of sympathetic audiences their stories of cruelty and depravity grew apace. Persecution and contempt from old friends increased their zeal. Birney, the Grimké sisters, Frederick Douglass, and many others influenced the movement and were influenced by it in a way comparable only to the relation of reformed drunkards to the temperance cause.

By means of such agencies and methods a well-defined picture of the South and slavery became slowly fixed in Northern minds. The Southern people were divided into two distinct classes—slaveholders and poor whites. The former constituted an aristocracy, living in great white-pillared houses on extended plantations. The latter, ignorant and impotent, made up a rural slum which clung hopelessly to the pine barrens or the worn-out acres on the fringes of the plantations. . . .

Social-economic conditions in the South were described as tumble-down and backward. The slave, lacking the incentive of personal gain, was inefficient. The master, ruined by power, self-indulgence, and laziness, was incapable of sound management. James Birney described the section as one

whose Agriculture is desolation—whose Commerce is mainly confined to a crazy wagon and half fed team of oxen or mules as a means of carrying it on—whose manufacturing "Machinery" is limited to the bones and sinews of reluctant slaves—whose currency is individual notes always to *be* paid (it may be at some broken bank) and mortgages on men and women and children who may run away or die, and on land, which without them is of little value. . . .

Others went so far as to charge the panic of 1837 to Southern profligacy. "The existence of Slavery," resolved the American Anti-Slavery Society in 1840, "is the grand cause of the pecuniary embarrassments of the country; and . . . no real or permanent relief is to be expected . . . until the total abolition of that execrable system." Joshua Leavitt called the slave system "a bottomless gulf of extravagance and thriftlessness." Another explained its "withering and impoverishing effect by the fact that it was the "rule of violence and arbitrary will. . . . It would be quite in character with its theory and practice," he said, "if slave-drivers should refuse to pay their debts and meet the sheriff with dirk and pistol." Leavitt estimated that the South had "taken from the North, within five years, more than $100,000,000, by notes which will never be paid," and quoted an English writer to the effect that "planters are always in debt. The system of society in a slaveholding community is such as to lead to the contraction of debt, which the system itself does not furnish the means of paying. . . ."

Nor did the Southern shortcomings, according to the anti-slavery view, end with things material. Moral weaknesses were even more offensive. Sexual virtue was scarcely known. "The Slave States," wrote an abolitionist, "are Sodoms, and almost every village family is a brothel." Another writer declared that "in the slaveholding settlements of Middle and Southern Mississippi . . . there [was] not a virtuous young man of twenty years of age." "To send a lad to a male academy in Mississippi," he said, "is moral murder." An anti-slavery pamphlet told of "a million and a half of slave women, some of them without even the tinge of African blood . . . given up a lawful prey to the unbridled lusts of their masters." Another widely circulated tract described a slave market in which one dealer "de-

voted himself exclusively to the sale of young mulatto women." The author pictured the sale of "the most beautiful woman I ever saw," without *"a single trace of the African about her features"* and with "a pair of eyes that pierced one through and through" to "one of the most lecherous-looking old brutes" that he had ever seen. The narrative closed with the shrieking appeal: "God shield the helpless victim of that bad man's power—it may be, ere now, that bad man's lust!" The conclusion was inescapable. Slavery and unrestrained sexual indulgence at Negro expense were inseparable.

In such a section and in the hands of such men, abolitionists assumed that slavery realized its most vicious possibilities. Anti-slavery men early set themselves to the task of collecting stories of cruelty. These were passed about from one to another, often gaining in ferocity as they travelled. Weld gathered them together in a volume entitled *American Slavery As It Is* and scattered them broadcast over the North. The annual reports of the anti-slavery societies, their tracts and periodicals, also revelled in atrocities, asking no more proof of their absolute truth than the word of a fellow fanatic.

The attempt to picture slavery "as it was," therefore, came to consist almost entirely of a recital of brutalities. Now and then a kind master and seemingly contented slaves were introduced for the purpose of contrast—as a device to deepen shadows. But, as a rule, Southerners, according to these tracts, spent their time in idleness broken only by brutal cockfights, gander pullings, and horse races so barbarous that "the blood of the tortured animal drips from the lash and flies at every leap from the stroke of the rowel." Slavery was one continual round of abuse. . . .

To abuse was added other great wrongs. Everywhere slaves were overworked, underfed, and insufficiently clothed and sheltered. Family ties were cut without the slightest regard for Negro feelings—infants were torn from the mother's breast, husbands separated from their wives and families. Marriage was unknown among slaves, and the right to worship God generally denied. Strangely enough, little was said of slave-breeding for market. That charge was largely left to the politicians of the next decades and to the historians of a later day.

Two principal assumptions stood out in this anti-slavery indictment of the slaveholder. He was, in the first place, the arch-aristocrat. He was the great enemy of democracy. He was un-American, the oppressor of his fellow men, the exploiter of a weaker brother. Against him could be directed all the complaints and fears engendered by industrial captains and land speculators. He, more than any other aristocrat, threatened to destroy the American democratic dream.

In the second place, he was a flagrant sinner. His self-indulgence was unmatched. His licentious conduct with Negro women, his intemperance in the use of intoxicating liquors, his mad dueling, and his passion for war against the weak were enough to mark him as the nation's moral enemy number one! The time for dealing moderately had passed. Immediate reform was imperative.

Thus it was that the slaveholder began to do scapegoat service for all aristocrats and all sinners. To him were transferred resentments and fears born out of local conditions. Because it combined in itself both the moral and the democratic appeal, and because it coincided with sectional rivalry, the abolition movement gradually swallowed up all other reforms. The South became the great object of all efforts to remake American society. Against early indifference and later persecution, a handful of deadly-in-earnest men and women slowly built into a section's consciousness the belief in a Slave Power. To the normal strength of sectional ignorance and distrust they added all the force of Calvinistic morality and American democracy and thereby surrounded every Northern interest and contention with holy sanction and reduced all opposition to abject depravity. When the politician, playing his risky game, linked expansion and slavery, Christian common folk by the thousands, with no great personal urge for reforming, accepted the Abolition attitudes toward both the South and slavery. Civil war was then in the making.

The conclusions of C. VANN WOODWARD
(1905–   ), Sterling Professor of History at Yale,
are not radically different from those of Craven.
Unlike Craven, however, Woodward raises the classical
question of means versus ends in a dramatic appraisal
of the reactions of Northern abolitionists to,
and the consequences of, John Brown's raid
on Harpers Ferry in 1859.*

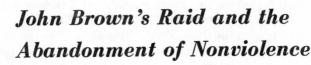

John Brown's Raid and the
Abandonment of Nonviolence

The figure John Brown is still wrapped in obscurity and myth. . . . His fifty-nine years were divided sharply into two periods. The obscurity of his first fifty-five years was of the sort natural to a humble life unassociated with events of importance. The obscurity of his last four years, filled with conspiratorial activities, was in large part the deliberate work of Brown, his fellow conspirators, and their admirers.

Poverty and failure haunted the first fifty-five years of John Brown's life. The father of twenty children, he was compelled to see his family drag along in want and at times in something approaching destitution. In thirty-five years

he was engaged in more than twenty different business ventures in six states. Most of them ended in failure, some in bankruptcy, and at least two in crime. Brown was involved for years as defendant in one litigation after an other brought against him for failure to meet his financial obligations. "Several of the cases in question leave no doubt of flagrant dishonesty on his part in both business and family relations," concludes Professor James C. Malin. The historian suggests that "this record of unreliability proven in court" might serve as "an index to the reliability of John Brown as a witness after he became a public character." The remarkable thing about this

* From C. Vann Woodward, "John Brown's Private War," reprinted from *America in Crisis* edited by Daniel Aaron, by permission of Alfred A. Knopf, Inc. Copyright © 1952 by Alfred A. Knopf, Inc. Pp. 110–130.

record is that it seems to have interfered in no way with the second of his careers. After 1855 John Brown abandoned his unprofitable business career when he was almost penniless and for the rest of his life was without remunerative employment. He depended for support upon donations from people whom he convinced of his integrity and reliability. Here and elsewhere there is strong evidence that Brown was somehow able to inspire confidence and intense personal loyalty.

The Kansas phase of Brown's guerrilla warfare has given rise to the "Legend of Fifty-six," a fabric of myth that has been subjected to a more rigorous examination than any other phase of Brown's life has ever received. Malin establishes beyond question that "John Brown did not appear to have had much influence either in making or marring Kansas history," that his exploits "brought tragedy to innocent settlers," but that "in no place did he appear as a major factor." He also establishes a close correlation between the struggle over freedom and slavery and local clashes over conflicting land titles on the Kansas frontier, and he points out that "the business of stealing horses under the cloak of fighting for freedom and running them off to the Nebraska-Iowa border for sale" is a neglected aspect of the struggle for "Bleeding Kansas." John Brown and his men engaged freely and profitably in this business and justified their plunder as the spoils of war. . . .

It would be a gross distortion, however, to dismiss John Brown as a frontier horse thief. He was much too passionately and fanatically in earnest about his war on slavery to permit of any such oversimplification. His utter fearlessness, courage, and devotion to the cause were greatly admired by respectable antislavery men who saw in the old Puritan an ideal revolutionary leader.

One exploit of Brown in Kansas, however, would seem to have put him forever beyond the pale of association with intelligent opponents of slavery. This was the famous Pottawatomie massacre of May 24, 1856. John Brown, leading four of his sons, a son-in-law, and two other men, descended by night upon an unsuspecting settlement of four proslavery families. Proceeding from one home to another the raiders took five men out, murdered them, and left their bodies horribly mutilated. None of the victims was a slaveholder, and two of them were born in Germany and had no contact with the South. By way of explanation Brown said the murders had been "decreed by Almighty God, ordained from Eternity." He later denied responsibility for the act, and some of the Eastern capitalists and intellectuals who supported him refused to believe him guilty. In view of the report of the murders that was laid before the country on July 11, 1856, in the form of a committee report in the House of Representatives, it is somewhat difficult to excuse such ignorance among intelligent men.

It was shortly after this report was published, however, that, for his war on slavery, Brown enjoyed his most striking success in soliciting contributions and making friends among men of wealth and intellectual distinction in Boston and other Eastern cities. In the first four months of 1858 he succeeding in raising $23,000 in cash, supplies, and credit to support his guerrilla activities.

In the spring of 1858 plans for a raid on Virginia began to take definite shape. To a convention of fellow conspirators in Chatham, Canada, in May, John Brown presented his remarkable "Provisional Constitution and Ordinances for the People of the United States." It represented the form of government he proposed to establish by force of arms with a handful of conspirators and an armed insurrection of slaves. Complete with legislative, executive, and judicial branches, Brown's revolutionary government was in effect a military dictatorship, since all acts of his congress had to be approved by the commander-in-chief of the army in order to become valid. Needless to say, John Brown was elected commander-in-chief.

By July, 1859, Commander-in-Chief Brown had established himself at a farm on the Maryland side of the Potomac River, four miles north of Harpers Ferry. There he assembled twenty-one followers and accumulated ammunition and other supplies, including 200 revolvers, 200 rifles, and 950 pikes specially manufactured for the slaves he expected to rise up in insurrection. On Sunday night, October 16, after posting a guard of three men at the farm, he set forth with eighteen followers, five of them Negroes, and all of them young men, to start his war of liberation and found his abolitionist republic. Brown's first objective, to capture the United States arsenal at Harpers Ferry, was easily accomplished since it was without military guard. In the Federal armory and the rifle works, also captured, were sufficient arms to start the bloodiest slave insurrection in history.

The commander-in-chief appears to have launched his invasion without any definite plan of campaign and then proceeded to violate every military principle in the book. He cut himself off from his base of supplies, failed to keep open his only avenues of retreat, dispersed his small force, and bottled the bulk of them up in a trap where defeat was inevitable. "In fact, it was so absurd," remarked Abraham Lincoln, "that the slaves, with all their ignorance, saw plainly enough it could not succeed." Not one of them joined Brown voluntarily, and those he impressed quickly departed. The insurrectionists killed one United States Marine and four inhabitants of Harpers Ferry, including the mayor and a Negro freeman. Ten of their own number, including two of Brown's sons, were killed, five were taken prisoner by a small force of Marines commanded by Robert E. Lee, and seven escaped, though two of them were later arrested. John Brown's insurrection ended in a tragic and dismal failure.

When news of the invasion was first flashed across the country, the most common reaction was that this was obviously the act of a madman, that John Brown was insane. This explanation was particularly attractive to Republican politicians and editors, whose party suffered the keenest embarrassment from the incident. Fall elections were on, and the new Congress was about to convene. Democrats immediately charged that John Brown's raid was the inevitable consequence of the "irresistable-conflict" and "higher-law" abolitionism preached by Republican leaders William H. Seward and Salmon P. Chase. "Brown's invasion," wrote Senator Henry Wilson of Massachusetts, "has thrown us, who were in a splendid position, into a defensive polition. . . . If we are defeated next year we shall owe it to that foolish and insane movement of Brown's." . . .

The insurrectionist himself, of course, stoutly maintained that he was perfectly sane, and he was certainly able to convince many intelligent people, both friend and foe, that he was sane. He firmly refused to plead insanity at his trial. Governor Henry A. Wise of Virginia went so far as to write out orders to the superintendent of the state insane asylum to examine Brown, but endorsed the orders, "countermanded upon reflection." On the other hand, John Brown pronounced Governor Wise mad. "Hard to tell who's mad," jested Wendell Phillips to a laughing congregation in Henry Ward Beecher's church. "The world says one man's mad. John Brown said the same of the Governor. . . . I appeal from Philip drunk to Philip sober." He meant future generations when, he said, "the light of civilization has had more time to penetrate." Then it would be plain that not Brown but his enemies were mad.

We, the Philips sober of the future, with some misgivings about how far "the light of civilization" has penetrated, do think we know a little more about insanity than did our great-grandfathers. We at least know that it is a loose expression for a variety of mental disorders and that it is a relative term. What seems sane to some people at some times seems insane to other people at other times. In our own time we have witnessed what we consider psychopathic personalities rise to power over millions of people and plunge the world into war. Yet to the milions who followed them these leaders appeared sublime in their wisdom. . . .

The prestige and character of the men who lent John Brown active, if sometimes secret, support likewise suggest caution in dismissing Harpers Ferry as merely the work of a madman. Among Brown's fellow conspirators the most notable were the so-called Secret Six. Far from being horse thieves and petty traders, the Secret Six came from the cream of Northern society. Capitalist, philan-

thropist, philosopher, surgeon, professor, minister—they were men of reputability and learning, four of them with Harvard degrees.

With a Harvard Divinity School degree, a knowledge of twenty languages, and a library of sixteen thousand volumes, Theodore Parker was perhaps the most prodigiously learned American of his time. In contant correspondence with the leading Republican politicians, he has been called "the Conscience of a Party." What Gerrit Smith, the very wealthy philanthropist and one-time congressman of Peterboro, New York, lacked in mental endowments he made up in good works—earnest efforts to improve the habits of his fellow men. These included not only crusades against alcohol and tobacco in all forms, but also coffee, tea, meat, and spices — "almost everything which gave pleasure," according to his biographer. Generous with donations to dietary reform, dress reform, woman's rights, educational and "non-resistance" movements, Smith took no interest whatever in factory and labor reform, but he was passionately absorbed in the antislavery movement and a liberal contributor to John Brown. Dr. Samuel G. Howe of Boston, husband of the famous Julia Ward Howe, was justly renowned for his humanitarian work for the blind and mentally defective. . . . The most generous man of wealth among the conspirators was George L. Stearns of Boston, a prosperous manufacturer of lead pipe. In the opinion of this revolutionary capitalist, John Brown was "the representative man of this century, as Washington was of the last." Finally there were two younger men, fledgling conspirators. The son of a prosperous Boston merchant who was bursar of Harvard, Thomas Wentworth Higginson became pastor of a church in Worcester after taking his divinity degree at Harvard. Young Franklin B. Sanborn was an apostle of Parker and a protégé of Emerson, who persuaded Sanborn to take charge of a school in Concord.

The most tangible service the Secret Six rendered the conspiracy lay in secretly diverting to John Brown, for use at Harpers Ferry, money and arms that had been contributed to the Massachusetts-Kansas Aid Committee for use in "Bleeding Kansas.". . .

Although they knew perfectly well the general purpose of Brown, the Secret Six were careful to request him not to tell them the precise time and place of the invasion. The wily old revolutionist could have told them much that they did not know about the psychology of fellow travelers. Brown had earlier laid down this strategy for conspirators who were hard pressed: "Go into the houses of your most prominent and influential white friends with your wives; and that will effectually fasten upon them the suspicion of being connected with you, and will compel them to make a common cause with you, whether they would otherwise live up to their professions or not." The same strategy is suggested by Brown's leaving behind, in the Maryland farmhouse where they would inevitably be captured, all his private papers, hundreds of letters of himself and followers, implicating nobody knew how many respectable fellow travelers.

When news of the captured documents arrived, there occurred a very unheroic panic among the Secret Six, who saw stark ruin and an indictment for treason facing them. Stearns, Sanborn, and Howe fled to Canada. Parker was already abroad. Gerrit Smith's secretary did not stop until he reached England. Smith himself issued pitiable and panicky denials of his guilt, then found refuge in insanity and was confined to an asylum. Howe published a denial unworthy of respect. Higginson alone stood his ground. Stearns and Howe denied any knowledge of the attack before a congressional committee, and both of them told Sanborn they "found the question of the Senate Committee so unskillfully framed that they could, without literal falsehood, answer as they did."

The assistance that the Secret Six conspirators were able to give John Brown and his Legend was as nothing compared with that rendered by other Northern intellectuals. Among them was the cultural and moral aristocracy of America in the period that has been called a "Renaissance." Some of these men, Ralph Waldo Emerson and Henry Thoreau among them, had met and admired Brown and even made small contributions to his cause. But they were safely beyond reproach of the law and were never taken into his confidence in the way that the Secret Six were. Their service was rendered after the event in justifying and glorifying Brown and his invasion.

In this work the intellectuals were ably assisted by a genius, a genius at self-justification—John Brown himself. From his prison cell he poured out a stream of letters, serene and restrained, filled with Biblical language and fired with overpowering conviction that his will and God's were one and the same. These letters and his famous speech at the trial constructed for the hero a new set of motives and plans and a new role. For Brown had changed roles. In October he invaded Virginia as a conqueror armed for conquest, carrying with him guns and pikes for the army he expected to rally to his standard and a new constitution to replace the one he overthrew. In that role he was a miserable failure. Then in November he declared at his trial: "I never did intend murder, or treason, or the destruction of property, or to excite or incite slaves to rebellion, or to make an insurrection." He only intended to liberate slaves without bloodshed, as he falsely declared he had done in Missouri the year before. How these statements can be reconciled with the hundreds of pikes, revolvers, and rifles, the capture of an armory, the taking of hostages, the killing of unarmed civilians, the destruction of government property, and the arming of slaves is difficult to see. Nor is it possible to believe that Brown thought he could seize a Federal arsenal, shoot down United States Marines, and overthrow a government without committing treason. "It was all so thin," as Robert Penn Warren has observed of the trial speech, "that it should not have deceived a child, but it deceived a generation." At Lincoln's funeral Emerson compared it with the Gettysburg Address.

Emerson seemed hesitant in his first private reactions to Harpers Ferry. Thoreau, on the other hand, never hesitated a moment. On the day after Brown's capture he compared the hero's inevitable execution with the crucifixion of Christ. Harpers Ferry was "the best news that America ever had"; Brown, "the bravest and humanest man in all the country," "a Transcendentalist above all," and he declared: "I rejoice that I live in this age, that I was his contemporary." Emerson quickly fell into line with Thoreau, and in his November 8 lecture on "Courage" described Brown as "the saint, whose fate yet hangs in suspense, but whose martyrdom, if it shall be perfected, will make the gallows as glorious as the cross."

Within a few weeks Emerson gave three important lectures, in all of which he glorified John Brown.

With the Sage of Concord and his major prophet in accord on the martyr, the majority of the transcendental hierarchy sooner or later joined in — William E. Channing, Bronson and Luisa May Alcott, Longfellow, Bryant, and Lowell, and of course Wendell Phillips and Theodore Parker. Parker pronounced Brown "not only a martyr . . . but also a SAINT." Thoreau and Henry Ward Beecher frankly admitted they hoped Brown would hang. To spare a life would be to spoil a martyr. They were interested in him not as a man but as a symbol, a moral ideal, and a saint for a crusade. In the rituals of canonization the gallows replaced the cross as a symbol. Louisa May Alcott called the gallows "a stepping-stone to heaven"; Parker, "the road to heaven"; Theodor Tilton, "a throne greater than a king's"; and Phillips concluded that "henceforth it is sacred forever."

Among Western antislavery men there were fewer intellectuals of fame or notoriety, but abolitionist preachers, teachers, and orators joined in apotheosizing Brown. Citizens of Oberlin erected a monument to three Negroes who gave their lives in Brown's raid. And Theodore D. Weld, once the genius of Western abolitionism, though in retirement, permitted burial of two of the Harpers Ferry raiders at his school in New Jersey. Not all of the Northern intellectuals became members of the Brown cult. Nathaniel Hawthorne and Walt Whitman were two notable dissenters. Devotees of the cult showed little tolerance for dissent. Emerson declared that "all people, in proportion to their sensibility and self-respect, sympathize with him [Brown]," and Thoreau carried intolerance to the point of moral snobbery. "When a noble deed is done, who is likely to appreciate it? They who are noble themselves," answered Thoreau. "I was not surprised that certain of my neighbors spoke of John Brown as an ordinary felon, for who are they? They have either much flesh, or much office, or much coarseness of some kind. They are not ethereal natures in any sense. The dark qualities predominate in them. . . . For the children of the light to contend with them is as if there should be a contest between eagles and owls."

The task to which the intellectuals of the cult dedicated themselves was the idealizing of John Brown as a symbol of the moral order and the social purpose of the Northern cause. Wendell Phillips expressed this best when he declared in the Boston Music Hall: " 'Law' and 'order' are only means for the halting ignorance of the last generation. John Brown is the impersonation of God's order and God's law, moulding a better future, and setting for it an example." In substituting the new revolutionary law and order for traditional law and order, the intellectuals encountered some tough problems in morals and values. It was essential for them to justify a code of political methods and morals that was at odds with the Anglo-American tradition. . . .

The crisis of Harpers Ferry was a crisis of means, not of ends. John Brown did not raise the question of whether slavery should be abolished or tolerated. That question had been raised in scores of ways and debated for a generation. Millions held strong convictions on the subject. Upon abolition, as an *end*, there was no difference between John Brown and the American and Foreign Anti-

Slavery Society. But as to the *means* of attaining abolition, there was as much difference between them, so far as the record goes, as there is between the modern British Labour Party and the government of Soviet Russia on the means of abolishing capitalism. The Anti-Slavery Society was solemnly committed to the position of nonviolent means. In the very petition that Lewis Tappan, secretary of the society, addressed to Governor Wise in behalf of Brown he repeated the rubric about "the use of all carnal weapons for deliverance from bondage." But in their rapture over Brown as martyr and saint the abolitionists lost sight of their differences with him over the point of means and ended by totally compromising their creed of nonviolence.

But what of those who clung to the democratic principle that differences should be settled by ballots and that the will of the majority should prevail? Phillips pointed out: "In God's world there are no majorities, no minorities; one, on God's side, is a majority." And Thoreau asked, "When were the good and the brave ever in a majority?" So much for majority rule. What of the issue of treason? The Reverend Fales H. Newhall of Roxbury declared that the word "treason" had been "made holy in the American language"; and the Reverend Edwin M. Wheelock of Boston blessed "the sacred, and the radiant 'treason' of John Brown."

No aversion to bloodshed seemed to impede the spread of the Brown cult. William Lloyd Garrison thought that "every slaveholder has forfeited his right to live" if he impeded emancipation. The Reverend Theodore Parker predicted a slave insurrection in which "The Fire of Vengeance" would run "from man to man, from town to town" through the South. "What shall put it out?" he asked. "The White Man's blood." The Reverend Mr. Wheelock thought Brown's "mission was to inaugurate slave insurrection as the divine weapon of the antislavery cause." He asked: "Do we shrink from the bloodshed that would follow?" and answered, "No such wrong [as slavery] was ever cleansed by rose-water." . . . In these pronouncements the doctrine that the end justifies the means had arrived pretty close to justifying the liquidation of an enemy class.

The reactions of the extremists have been stressed in part because it was the extremist view that eventually prevailed in the apotheosis of John Brown and, in part, because by this stage of the crisis each section tended to judge the other by the excesses of a few. "Republicans were all John Browns to the Southerners," as Professor Dwight L. Dumond has observed, "and slaveholders were all Simon Legrees to the Northerners." As a matter of fact Northern conservatives and unionists staged huge anti-Brown demonstrations that equaled or outdid those staged by the Brown partisans. Nathan Appleton wrote a Virginian: "I have never in my long life seen a fuller or more enthusiastic demonstration" than the anti-Brown meeting in Faneuil Hall in Boston. The Republican press described a similar meeting in New York as "the largest and most enthusiastic" ever held in that city. Northern politicians of high rank, including Lincoln, Douglas, Seward, Edward Everett, and Henry Wilson, spoke out against John Brown and his methods. The Republican party registered its official position by a plank in the 1860 platform denouncing the Harpers Ferry raid. Lincoln approved of Brown's execution, "even though he agreed with us in thinking slavery wrong." Agreement on ends did not mean agreement on means. "That cannot excuse violence, bloodshed, and treason," said Lincoln. . . .

Among the Brown partisans not one has been found but who believed that Harpers Ferry had resulted in great gain for the extremist cause. So profoundly were they convinced of this that they worried little over the conservative dissent. "How vast the change in men's hearts!" exclaimed Phillips. "Insurrection was a harsh, horrid word to millions a month ago." Now it was "the lesson of the hour." Garrison rejoiced that thousands who could not listen to his gentlest rebuke ten years before "now easily swallow John Brown whole, and his rifle in the bargain." "They all called him crazy then," wrote Thoreau; "Who calls him crazy now?" To the poet it seemed that "the North is suddenly all Transcendentalist." On the day John Brown was hanged church bells were tolled in commemoration in New England towns, out along the Mohawk Valley, in Cleveland and the Western Reserve, in Chicago and northern Illinois. In Albany one hundred rounds were fired from a cannon. Writing to his daughter the following day, Joshua Giddings of Ohio said, "I find the hatred of slavery greatly intensified by the fate of Brown and men are ready to march to Virginia and dispose of her despotism at once." It was not long before they *were* marching to Virginia, and marching to the tune of "John Brown's Body."

The Harpers Ferry crisis on the other side of the Potomac was a faithful reflection of the crisis in the North, and can therefore be quickly sketched. It is the reflection, with the image reversed in the mirror, that antagonistic powers present to each other in a war crisis. To the

South John Brown also appeared as a true symbol of Northern purpose, but instead of the "angel of light" Thoreau pictured, the South saw an angel of destruction. The South did not seriously question Brown's sanity either, for he seemed only the rational embodiment of purposes that Southern extremist had long taught were universal in the North. The crisis helped propagandists falsely identify the whole North with John Brownism. For Harpers Ferry strengthened the hand of extremists and revolutionists in the South as it did in the North, and it likewise discredited and weakened moderates and their influence.

The risk one runs in describing the reaction to Harpers Ferry is the risk of attributing to that event tendencies long manifest. The South had been living in a crisis atmosphere for a long time. It was a society in the grip of an insecurity complex, a tension resulting from both rational and irrational fears. One cause of it was the steady, invincible expansion of the free-state system in size and power, after the Southern system had reached the limits of its own expansion. The South, therefore, felt itself to be menaced through encirclement by a power containing elements unfriendly to its interests, elements that were growing strong enough to capture the government. The South's insecurity was heightened by having to defend against constant attack an institution it knew to be discredited throughout the civilized world and of which Southerners had once been among the severest critics. Its reaction was to withdraw increasingly from contact with the offending world, to retreat into an isolationism of spirit, and to attempt by curtailing freedom of speech to avoid criticism.

One of the South's tensions sprang from a lack of internal security—the fear of servile insurrection. . . . It is significant that two of the most severe panics of this sort occurred in the election years 1856 and 1860 and were accompanied by charges that abolitionists from the North were fomenting uprisings. Harpers Ferry was therefore a blow at the most sensitive area of Southern consciousness.

The first reaction to the raid, outside Virginia, was surprisingly mild. . . . This mood did not last long, however. The hundreds of captured documents belonging to Brown and his men persuaded Virginia authorities that the conspiracy was widespread and that the Harpers Ferry strike, had it been successful, was intended to be merely the signal for uprisings throughout the South. . . .

Letters from all parts of the South deluged Governor Wise's mail with reports that Brown conspirators had been seized or punished. These, and the Southern newspaper of the time, portray a society in the throes of panic. Convinced that the South was honeycombed with subversives, Southerners tended to see an abolitionist behind every bush and a slave insurrection brewing in the arrival of any stranger. Victims of vigilante and mob action ranged from aged eccentrics and itinerant piano-tuners to substantial citizens of long residence. The mob spirit was no respecter of person or class. A sixty-year-old minister in Texas, who was a believer in the Biblical sanction of slavery and a Democrat of Kentucky birth, made the mistake of criticizing the treatment of slaves in a sermon and was given seventy lashes on his back. A schoolteacher who had lived in Louisiana and Arkansas for ten years was given thirty-six hours to leave the latter state. The newly arrived president of an Alabama college, who came from New York, was forced to give up his job and flee for his life. In December, 1859, twelve families, including thirty-nine people associated with antislavery schools and churches of Berea, Kentucky, were forcibly expelled from the state for abolitionism.

Southern fire-eaters swore that no Northerner could be trusted and that all should be expelled. Even the humblest workmen from the North were in danger of insult, violence, or lynching. An Irish stonecutter in Columbia, South Carolina, was beaten, tarred and feathered, and expelled from the state by a mob. Three members of the crew of a brig from Maine were brutally flogged in Georgia, and a New England mechanic was driven out of a village in the same state because he was found to have a clean shirt wrapped in a New York paper containing one of Beecher's sermons. Two Connecticut book-peddlers were roughly handled in Charleston when lists of slaves were found in their bags, and two printers were ridden out of Kingstree, South Carolina, on rails. . . . Not only Northerners but associates of Northerners were subject to persecution, for guilt by association was an accepted principle in the crisis. . . .

Southern zealots of secession had no better ally than John Brown. Robert B. Rhett, Edmund Ruffin, and William L. Yancey all rejoiced over the effect of Harpers Ferry. Nonslaveholders saw dramatized before them the menace of a slave uprising and readily concluded that their wives and children, as much as the home of the planter, were threatened with the horror of insurrection. They frequently became more fanatical secessionists than the planters. In face of the Northern apotheosis of Brown there was little that Southern moderates could say in answer to such pronouncements as that of the New Orleans *Picayune* of December 2: "Crime becomes godliness,

and criminals, red from the slaughter of innocent, are exalted to eminence beside the divine gospel of Peace." . . .

The crisis psychology of 1859 persisted and deepened in the fateful year of 1860 into a pathological condition of mind in which delusions of persecution and impending disaster flourished. Out of Texas came wild rumors of incendiary fires, abolitionists plotting with slaves, and impending insurrection on a vast scale. Rumors of large stocks of strychnine in the possession of slaves and of plans for well-poisoning were widely believed, though unproved. One scholar has aptly compared the tension of the South in 1860 with the "Great Fear" that seized the rural provinces of France in the summer of 1789 when panic spread the word that "the brigands are coming." In that atmosphere the South made the momentous decision that split the Democratic Party at Charleston in April, and before the mood was gone it was debating secession.

In the course of the crisis each of the antagonists, according to the immemorial pattern, had become convinced of the depravity and diabolism of the other. Each believed itself persecuted, menaced. "Let the 'higher law' of abolitionism be met by the 'higher law' of self-perservation," demanded the Richmond *Enquirer*. Lynch law was the only answer to pikes. "What additional insults and outrages *will* arouse it [the North] to assert its rights?" demanded Garrison. And Garrison's opposite number in Mississippi, Albert Gallatin Brown, cried: "Oh, God! To what depths of infamy are we sinking in the South if we allow these things to pass." Paranoia continued to induce counterparanoia, each antagonist infecting the other reciprocally, until the vicious spiral ended in war.

RUSSELL B. NYE (1915–   ), professor of English
at Michigan State University, rejects the idea
that the abolitionists were irresponsible fanatics
who precipitated a needless war. According to him,
they were farsighted realists who awakened the North
to the danger slavery presented to traditional
American principles of democracy and constitutional
government.*

Farsighted Reformers

The keynote of the abolitionist histories of the antebellum period, and of
the literature produced by the abolitionist movement, was the thesis that the
fight against slavery was not only a struggle to free the Negro from bondage, but
one to remove as a dominant force in
American life the threat of a well-
organized, aggressive, threatening "Slave
Power conspiracy," or what is called
"Slaveocracy." For the abolitionists, who
remained a minority in the North
throughout the entire pre-war period,
the "Slave Power threat" served as an
invaluable device in gaining public support. There was, they charged, a tacit
secret agreement among Southern slave-

holders not only to maintain undisturbed
their "peculiar institution," but to foist
it on the nation by extending it to the
territories and free states (possibly to
whites), to destroy civil liberties, control
the policies of the Federal government,
and complete the formation of a nation-
wide ruling aristocracy based on a slave
economy.

To many in the North who were relatively uninterested in the Negro's freedom, the appeal of the charge was strong.
Mechanics, immigrant laborers, farmers
and lower- and middle-class workmen,
prone to suspect the motives of the rich
and powerful, found in the abolitionist
contention more logic than is usually

* Russell B. Nye, "The Slave Power Conspiracy, 1830–1860," *Science and Society*, X (Summer,
1946), 262–274. Reprinted without footnotes by permission of *Science and Society*. Copyright © 1946
by *Science and Society*.

supposed. During the thirties the abolitionists warned constantly of the existence of such a conspiratorial movement
to crush liberty, though the term "Slave
Power" did not come into wide use until
the fifties. In 1839 the National Convention of Abolitionists, meeting at Albany,
resolved that "the events of the last five
or six years leave no room for doubt that
the SLAVE POWER is now waging a deliberate and determined war against the liberties of the free states," and by 1845
repetitions of the charge became common. From that date on Northern opinion was subjected to an increasing bar-
rage of proof, and began to be colored
appreciably by acceptance of it. As the
fear of "black Republicanism" and mis-
cegenation was used by the pro-slavery
element to unify Southern opinion, so
the genuine threat of the Slave Power
became an important factor in consolidating anti-slavery sentiment in the
North.

What was the Slave Power of which the
abolitionist warned, and from what conditions did it arise? A typical definition
called it "that control in and over the
government which is exercised by a com-
paratively small number of persons . . .
bound together in a common interest, by
being owners of slaves"; all definitions
agreed that it was fundamentally "an
aristocracy constituted and organized on
the basis of ownership of slaves." Its
origins lay in the institution of slavery.
. . . The threat of Slave Power domina-
tion was intensified, said the abolitionists, by the danger of a coalition of Southern slaveholder and Northern capitalist
to form a ruling oligarchy. The two had
certain moral affinities and a clear identity of interest, it was pointed out, and
concerted action was logical and immi-
nent. The tendency to include in the

term "Slave Power" not only slaveholders
but also Northern industrialists grew,
until by 1850 the term meant, as Wendell Phillips strikingly phrased it, an
alliance of "the Lords of the Lash and
the Lords of the Loom." "The wealth of
the North and the wealth of the South,"
cried The Antislavery Bugle, "are combined to crush the liberal, free progressive spirit of the age," and the fight
against the Slave Power became a battle
against conservatism, reaction, aristocracy, and the power of capital—in Ohio
and Massachusetts as well as in South
Carolina.

It was not difficult for the abolitionists
to recruit evidence to prove that there
actually was a Slave Power conspiracy.
After 1850, when they began to publicize
the charge in earnest, they interpreted
the drift of recent events in the light of
its existence. Joshua Giddings of Ohio,
writing in the forties, listed ten proofs
from history to substantiate the belief
that a well-organized Southern slaveholding cabal had operated in the past,
and might again: the fugitive slave law
of 1793, the Creek-Negro troubles in
Florida in 1815, the Seminole War, the
maintenance of slavery in the District of
Columbia, the controversy over the mails
and petitions in Congress in 1836, attacks
on free speech and press, and demands
for extension of the slavery to the Southwest and for the reopening of the slave
trade. Seward in 1855 added the Missouri
Compromise, the annexation of Texas,
the Mexican War, the Kansas struggle,
and the 1850 Compromise to the list of
Slave Power victories. The Dred Scott
case clinched the evidence, and by 1858
a substantial number of Northerners
were ready to believe, as did the non-
abolitionist Cincinnati Daily Commercial of March 12, 1857, that "There is

such a thing as the SLAVE POWER. It has marched over and annihilated the boundaries of the states. We are now one great homogeneous slaveholding community." The aim of this conspiracy, whose existence was thus established, was threefold: to reopen the slave trade; to extend slavery throughout the entire nation and beyond; and, most dangerous threat of all, to make the free white man a virtual slave to a privileged aristocracy of Southern slaveholder and Northern capitalist.

Southern agitation after 1850 for the renewal of the slave trade lent rather convincing proof to the first claim. The failing slave economy led many Southerners to advocate a revival of slave importations as the only remedy for the South's economic difficulties, and abolitionists seized upon the argument as evidence that the Slave Power intended to entrench itself even more firmly by thus bolstering the institution upon which it rested. In the years following, Southern demands became more insistent and frequent (a marked illustration of how completely the South had become committed to the defense and maintenance of slavery) while the abolitionist press kept careful watch of ruses, such as proposals to import "indentured" Negroes, Negro apprentices, or to form "African Labor Importation Associations." The loosening of the 1808 laws against the slave trade or their repeal, warned the abolitionists, would result without doubt in a new and doubly potent Slave Power.

Stressed more strongly by the abolitionists and supported by more substantial evidence was the claim that the Slave Power intended to establish slavery on a nationwide and possibly a hemispheric basis. Gamaliel Bailey in 1844 exposed "a deliberate plot . . . to sustain the slavery of this country . . . and to extend it

over almost illimitable regions," and for more than a decade the press reported a boast by Toombs of Georgia that he would some day call the roll of his slaves on Bunker Hill. Furthermore, the abolitionist could cite the Kansas troubles, the attacks on anti-slavery men in the North, the Mexican War, Texas, the various Congressional compromises, the argument over slavery in the territories, and a host of other proofs. . . .

More difficult to establish, but tremendously effective as a propaganda issue, was the accusation that the Slave Power aimed eventually to subvert the liberties of white men, and to introduce virtual white slavery as national policy. Since slavery, reasoned the abolitionists was founded upon a violation of the principles of liberty and free government, it followed that by the simple fact of its existence slavery was a constant threat to those principles. Abolitionists had warned from the beginning that the Slave Power would some day crush white rights as it had black. . . .

II

It was not difficult to perceive the implications of the pro-slavery argument. If slavery were a positive good, superior to free society as an economic, political, and social system, it was reasonable to assume that the next step of its proponents would be to impose it upon the nation at large. . . . The slave laws made no distinction in color; slavery was a matter of condition alone. If a person who was 99.9% white could, under the law, be claimed as a slave, the next step was a logical one. The only reason for the existence of pigmentation as a basis for slavery, warned the abolitionist, was simply that the Negro, who because of his helpless condition could be made a slave, happened to have a different color. The truth was that the institution did not rest upon a distinction of race at all; "Where is the man," asked William Goodell, "who may not at any moment become a slave?" that is, if slavery is founded not upon color, but upon the right of the strong to enslave the weak?

In making their charges, the abolitionists made a particular effort to point out to the immigrant and the laborer, the two groups most likely to respond, the great stake they held in the abolition of slavery and the consequent defeat of the Slave Power. "American slavery," resolved the Massachusetts Antislavery Society in 1843, "is the deadliest foe of the rights of labor, and ought, therefore, to be the object of special indignation and alarm to the hardworking Irish immigrant." . . . Involuntary servitude, it was warned, could legally be made a prerequisite to citizenship, and by some such device the Slave Power might introduce white slavery for the foreign-born. As evidence, the abolitionists pointed to those provisions of the Nebraska bill which denied citizenship to territorial aliens for five years, and to the anti-foreign riots attendant to the Know-nothing movement. In general, the reaction of the foreign press, especially in the areas of German settlement, was sympathetic, while the influence of men such as C. C. Follen and Carl Schurz, both anti-slavery leaders, turned many immigrants toward the anti-slavery cause. Yet in the end it was not the Slave Power threat which enlisted the support of the foreign born in abolitionism, but other factors, primarily economic and political, and after 1856 and the decline of the nativistic troubles, the abolitionist campaign to convince the immigrant of the threat of white slavery was largely written off.

More successful was the appeal to the laboring classes. The workman, though little interested in the humanitarian aspects of the slavery question, intuitively perceived that his own liberties were to some extent involved in the issue. The existence of a slave labor system threatened his own status, and he could readily see that the competition of skilled and unskilled slaves tended to depreciate the value of free labor. . . .

Nearly the whole structure of the pro-slavery argument could be turned to support the abolitionist contention that the Southern Slave Power intended to enslave white laborers. . . . Such, said the abolitionist, was the intent of the Slave Power, and, if it gained political control of the federal government, it could realize its aim. It was not difficult to find and publicize extremely significant statements from the South. The Republican party in 1856 distributed a reprint of a South Carolina paper's belief that "Slavery is the natural state and normal condition of the laboring man, black or white." . . . Neither were such sentiments restricted to the South. Solon Robinson of Indiana, a prominent agricultural authority, defended slavery as "a perfect labor system" and suggested its adoption on the nation's farms, a view that found some agreement in Ohio and Illinois. The Salem *Register,* the Pittsburgh *Post,* the New York *Herald* and the extremely Southern New York *Day Book* thought slavery superior as a labor system, while in factory-conscious New England a debate was held on the question. The abolitionist claim that the extension of slavery to white labor was something more than an impossible chimera had a point, and evidence to buttress it. If slavery were ever extended to include whites, the laborer, since his political and economic position was weakest, would be the first to be enslaved—a fact the abolitionists never allowed the laborer to forget. Thus, in 1839, *The Emancipator* summarized the issue: "The struggle is between the antagonist principles of free and slave labor. They cannot much longer co-exist. One must prevail to the exclusion of the other. The laborers will either be free, or enslaved." Subsequent argument directed at Northern labor by the abolitionists deviated but little from this line, and they continued their appeal to the labor interests for assistance against the Slave Power until the Civil War.

Although the laboring class was too disorganized and too politically immature during the period to exert much influence, nevertheless in the main the effect of the abolitionist warnings of the Slave Power threat to its liberties was relatively large. . . . But though laboring interests, divided as they were, could give the abolitionist movement little organized assistance, the long campaign to convince the laborer of the Slave Power threat brought individual support to the anti-slavery cause, and bore material fruit when, in the form of the Republican party, it entered its political phase.

III

The abolitionist contention, that there existed a Slave Power conspiracy which threatened the continuation of liberty, was an important factor in enlisting support among certain Northern elements for the anti-slavery movement. In some ways, and in some groups, the "great Slave Power plot" overshadowed in importance the religious, humanitarian, moral, and political issues of the controversy. The claim tended to discredit the pro-slavery argument, reading into it sinister implications; by carrying Southern logic to its ultimate conclusion and by identifying the slaveholder with a conspiracy of infinitely dangerous designs, the abolitionists robbed the pro-slavery position of any possible appeal to the immigrant, the workman, and the lower middle class in the North. Then too, the Slave Power threat helped widen the rift between North and South by making it more difficult than ever to be neutral toward or tolerant of slavery or its extension. Neutrality or tolerance, said the abolitionist, implied lack of interest in or positive hostility to the preservation of the liberal, democratic tradition. The issue simply admitted of no compromise. Identifying their cause with the greater cause of liberty, with republican government, and with the interests of large relatively unorganized special groups such as laborers or immigrants, the abolitionists made theirs the cause of civil and political freedom. The Slave Power threat personified the pro-slavery argument, made it vivid and concrete, and dramatized the controversy into a contest between good and evil, freedom and oppression, democracy and aristocracy. When war came, it was justified by the abolitionists and others as the last phase of the contest, as the final defense against the assaults of the Slave Power on traditional American rights. The South waged war, it was said, ". . . not against Abolitionism or Republicanism *per se,* but against free institutions and the democratic theory of government." Had it not been for the abolitionists, who awakened the people to the "villainous purposes and character of the Slave Power," we should have had "a nation in which were only two classes, *masters* and *slaves*."

Was there a Slave Power, and were the abolitionists correct in ascribing to it the evil designs which formed so large and important a part of the abolitionist propaganda? In the sense of the term as used by Wilson, Goodell, Bailey, Garrison, and others—a secret and highly organized group with conscious aims of imposing restrictions upon traditional liberties— the Slave Power conspiracy probably had no real existence. The South was never so completely unified as to warrant evidence of a definite "conspiracy.". . . However, it is clear that among Southern leaders there was unity of belief that

Slavery was a good system, probably the best, and that it should be retained and extended; the events of the period from 1830 to 1860 showed that in preserving and extending it the South was willing to infringe upon basic civil and personal rights, free speech, free press, free thought, and constitutional liberty. . . . While the "conspiracy" of which the abolitionists warned was no doubt a natural alliance of common political and economic interests, its threat to liberty, North and South, was more than idle. . . . and the abolitionists were not so far wrong in believing that its existence seriously jeopardized, for the first time since the founding of the republic, the American tradition.

STANLEY M. ELKINS (1925–   ), associate professor
of American history at Smith College, disagrees with
the conclusions of Craven, Woodward, and Nye.
Like them he concludes that the "estrangement
of North and South over slavery" led to secession
and war in 1861. But he takes issue with the idea
that the moral urgency of the slavery question
made war inevitable and the view that the Civil War
was a needless conflict caused by the reckless
fanaticism of Northern abolitionists. The real
difficulty, Elkins argues, lay in the absence of strong
national institutions in the United States during
the antebellum period.*

The Anti-institutional Character
of American Society

It is of the nature of tragedy that while
the choices it offers are most sharply and
painfully limited, such choices must still
exist. Were this not so, situations which
we call "tragic" would have little analy-
tic merit and no dramatic essence. It can
hardly be doubted that the estrangement
of North and South over slavery, and the
consequences of it, offer us what is po-
tentially the most distinguished subject
available in our history. That it might
have ended otherwise is a shadowy possibility that will trouble our minds forever. That there may have been alternatives—that choices were at least conceivable—makes it a subject not quite fore-
ordained and fatal, but tragic.

What openings might there have been
for intellectuals and agitators to play
meaningful roles in the controversy?
What specific alternatives might they
have pressed for? "Moderation" was not
really an alternative; the difficulty was
not harshness of tone; "moderate abolition" would mean nothing at all. The
true difficulty lay in the absence of any
sense of the *limits* within which the problem would have to be handled, limits
functioning to exhibit not only the impossible but also the possible. Yet in the
1830's those limits, for anyone really
looking for them, would not have been
very hard to find.

The major limit was the fact of slav-

* Reprinted from *Slavery: A Problem in American Institutional and Intellectual Life* by
Stanley M. Elkins without footnotes by permission of The University of Chicago Press. Copyright
© 1959 by The University of Chicago. Pp. 193–206.

ery's expansion in the Southwest and the commitment of this area, more than any other, to slave labor. There was no way of side-stepping such a fact as this; it would be the basic thing that reformers would be working with. Here was the area in which the reformer would have to expect abuse for virtually everything he said; it was here that he would make the least difference. The second fact, however, was that in other areas of the South —in the older planting states—an earlier commitment to slavery had been to some extent undermined during the first quarter of the century. Distinctions, that is, would have to be made; the slaveholding South could not realistically be considered a unit. It was here (in Virginia, North Carolina, Kentucky) that the system's weaknesses would be most exposed to whatever reform activity was feasible. The final test of the problem's limits was to be found in the deep hostility still existing at that time, not merely in the South but in the North itself, toward out-and-out abolitionism. The potential explosiveness of that issue, taken as a whole, was a thing recognized somehow by almost everyone. Potential support for a concrete policy would have to be calculated with this in mind.

What it all pointed to, if the system were eventually to be removed without bloodshed, was a catalogue of preliminaries—a series of separate short-term reforms rather than root-and-branch abolition. It is not difficult to conceive a few of the specific measures which might have been advanced. One such project, and here the national church organizations could afford to be implacable, would be that of bringing the slave into the Christian fold and under the eye of the church, of insisting that he be offered a spiritual life marked by dignity and be given instruction in Christian morality. For the slave, such arrangements would have functioned not merely as personal consolation but also as institutional leverage, as a claim on society. This tradition in the Latin [American] states impresses us by its subversive effects upon slavery, and we are struck, on the other hand, by the buffoonery, the lack of dignity and moral power, which characterizes much of the legend of plantation religion in our own South. The sanctity of the family could have been insisted upon as a basic principle of Christian practice, not simply to decrease personal anguish, but to establish another level of human dignity that society would, in some sense or other, be called upon to recognize. Conversely, were it a matter of official doctrine (as it was in Latin America) that the slave, for all his servile degradation, had been endowed with a moral personality as sacred as his master's, such precepts as those touching Christian marriage could hardly have been taken so lightly. There might have been a movement to write into law the best Southern practice as to the treat-treatment of the slave's person—not only to mitigate personal cruelty but to establish still a further claim, institutionally formalized before all society, for the slave's humanity. . . . Arrangements might further have been proposed for a program of incentives—such as the slave's use of free time to accumulate his purchase price, or freedom for meritorious service—which might, from the master's own point of view, improve the system. Such a policy might not noticeably improve the slave's own "standard of living," but it would set up formal channels of communication between himself and free society which were not previously there.

The presence of all these things in Latin America gives a clear indication of what might have been the consequences for the Negro community had they existed in this country. . . . By humanizing the Negro, by making property-holding legal, by regularizing procedures of manumission, social space would be provided; there would be a basis for the emergence of a Negro elite of leadership. A series of contacts with free society would thus have been established, and in such a setting many of the difficulties of a general emancipation, should such an event some day occur, would have been absorbed in advance. . . .

Actually, there was not a single one of these schemes that was not proposed in some form or other during the pre-Civil War generation and that has not been repeatedly considered by historians ever since. Indeed, the British example was there for anyone concerned with procedure; theirs was a program very similar to the one just outlined; their approach in softening up the system for final emancipation followed a pattern much resembling that just suggested.

And yet the setting made all the difference. It is one thing to point out that such proposals were there and quite another to find a setting in the America of the 1830's capable of receiving them, of testing them, of debating them, of transforming them into something more than mere proposals. It is something of a shock to realize that one cannot imagine a setting within which, for example, the proposals of Channing could be approached as a reasoned body of doctrine rather than as moral formulas, or in which it would have seemed natural to contrast Virginia and Mississippi, rather than North and South, with regard to slavery and its liabilities. The institution-

ally formed habits of mind needed to appraise the tactics of the British abolitionists were available neither to Garrison nor to other Americans interested in antislavery. . . . In contrast to the British antislavery program, whose every item was hammered out by daily experience over a period of years, any concrete proposal made by an American could only be thrown into the void.

For it to have been otherwise, a myriad of intermediate relationships would have been required. The reformers might have taken as their standards the standards of the best Southern families. What might this have had to offer the slaveowner of the older planting states who still felt guilt over his position as a holder of slaves? It could offer him a clear role as model slaveholder, a role which would have had at least one manifest function and two hidden ones. Not only would it carry prestige and general recognition, but it might also provide constructive channels for his sense of guilt and at the same time set the pattern for the system's ultimate dissolution. It was precisely here—not in the cotton kingdom but in the border states and older seaboard slave areas—that an enormously sensitive spot existed. On the one hand it made little sense to put economic pressure on the planters of these states, and on the other it was folly to accuse them of sin and make them guiltier. Incentives for taking action could never result from any such pressures. But moral incentives for improvement (rather than naked abolition) could operate quite differently since here the system was a good deal less secure than in Alabama and Mississippi. It was in such an area that reform might most effectively be generated. It was here, for instance, that colonization had made the greatest headway;

it was in this area, even, that actual antislavery activity, before the rise of Northern abolitionism, had been most prominent.

The resources of intellect and experience available to each shade of emancipationist feeling, from Massachusetts to Virginia, might have been considerable had there been some cultural matrix capable of containing them all. To operate with purpose and meaning in such a situation, the intellectual and reforming publicist would certainly have needed not only to know of but to understand the experience being undergone at that same period by the British. The intellectual's role would also have involved knowing what was happening to the slave system in Latin America, and having some rough idea of the reasons. It would further have involved a relationship to the humane slaveholder which need not inevitably have been one of "friendly sympathy" but would certainly have had to be one of responsibility, of sensitivity to his requirements. . . .

Had the national churches remained united and sensitive to the uses of power, it might have made considerable difference as to the choices made by religious groups in the matter of slavery. The Lane Seminary debate of the mid-1830's, for example—what was the nature of the choice made there? The students had begun the famous meeting by reasoning together, by questioning, with prayerful inquiry, into the nature of their moral duty. Might they not have arrived at a different decision? Suppose they had still resolved to go out in the service of Christ, as they conceived it, and to labor for the slave's welfare, but not as abolitionists? The Southern brethren might then have gone into the South, there announcing that on no account were they to be con-

fused with abolitionists, that their unshakable purpose was simply to bring Christ to the slave and to minister to the needs of his soul. . . . But of course there was no setting in which they could do this, in which they might say, evil is with us and we must work with it. They could not actually think of the slave in his present condition; they could only be overwhelmed by the sense of sin and guilt of slaveholding. Thus was stifled any sense they may have had of the needs of souls other than their own. More than Garrison it was they who, with the revival that followed, would find the formula—sin and guilt—that would drive the entire South in the same direction. . . .

What it all came to, finally, was that every such alternative became unreal, if not impossible. What made it so?

In every "tragic" situation a set of choices exists which might conceivably bring the conflict to a solution. Suppose Hamlet had destroyed his uncle in the first act? Suppose Othello had made his own investigations? But now let us admit that such questions, though by no means idle, have running through them a touch of the academic. To ask them is to confirm the rules of tragedy but also to contravene them, because in tragedy two elements are in mortal but uneven conflict: one involves the choices that exist; the other involves the circumstances which predispose the principals to choose one set of alternatives rather than another. It is with the latter that we must finally make our terms.

A recurrent theme in our histories continues to affront us: their intimation that the failure of American society to solve the problem of slavery without bloodshed was somehow the failure of men to curb their passions—that it was in some sense a breaking-loose of Northern radicalism and Southern fire-eating, a matter of too much "slogan-making" and "propaganda" (as the late Professor Randall put it) and not enough "moderation and understanding." But a healthy culture can afford this. Indeed, such a culture must have its fanaticism and moral passion in order that its moderation and sagacity may be given point and meaning. We should say that the difficulty lay elsewhere—that the great falling-short in American society was precisely its lack of proper channels for the launching either of its passion or its moderation, either of its propaganda, its slogan-making, or its deepest counsels of understanding.

There was no church with a national scope, which in its concern with the nation's morals would be forced to operate on intersectional terms. There were no national universities to focus intellectual activity, no intellectual matrix within which the most pressing problems of the day would have had to be debated on national grounds and on their merits. There was no national focus of social and financial power (the only possible American equivalent to a ruling class): no national vested business interest such as a national bank (the nearest approach to such a thing had been smashed during the Jackson administration); no established mercantile axis powerful enough to resist a sectional movement; no seaboard social axis reaching from Boston to Charleston, whose vested loyalties might have gone deeper than local ones. There was no national bar which would, with its vested interests in standards, be forced to meet the legal complications of slavery in a national way. Indeed, there were not even sectional (to say nothing of national) abolition societies—no organization which carried anything resembling power, or which lasted long enough to

accomplish anything against slavery. . . .

Very different was the case in England. There, no matter what men did, they did it in a setting in which they could hardly avoid thinking and acting institutionally. They behaved this way whether oppressing their poor or reforming their factories, manipulating their rotten boroughs or organizing their Reform Bills, massacring Peterloo "rabble" or celebrating Christmas Eve at Oxford and Westminster. . . . There was the Church of England, which reached deep into the daily life of every community and which also managed the ceremonial of the greatest occasion of state. Alongside it stood the noncomforming sects, which themselves maintained strong national establishments. There were the national universities (behind which stood the great public schools) through which was funneled a substantial portion of the future leaders in all areas of the national life. There was the ruling class, fluid enough in its recruitment to maintain its vitality, whose appurtenances of power, exhibited in a hundred ways, were yet clear enough to command the recognition of all society. It was the class through which all major matters of policy had to be channeled, and it had great independence in shaping the form in which such policy would emerge. There was a tradition of bench and bar, emanating from the King's Bench, with a set of customs, standards, training, and a body of law, all reaching far back into British experience—a tradition which made it not only possible, but natural, that men should conceive the actual terms upon which law would be put into practice at the very time such law was being enacted. The elites of these and other institutions crossed one another's paths a dozen times a year. All this, in terms of social structure, was of course what James had in mind in his "lurid indictment" of the United States: "No sovereign, no court . . . no aristocracy, no church . . . no great universities nor public schools— no Oxford, nor Eton, nor Harrow; . . . No political society, no sporting class— no Epsom nor Ascot!"

The antislavery movement in England had an array of resources, and habits of mind appropriate to them, which were in no way available to Americans. The differences between the two movements were no mere differences of formula (the formulas themselves were superficially similar); the crucial differences were those which existed between two cultures.

The British abolitionists made use of every institution, every center of power, that they had at hand. The movement had a continuity of leadership which dated from the initial agitation against the slave trade in the 1780's and re-mained intact until the final abolition of slavery itself in the 1830's. . . .

The "immediate emancipation" form-ula which Garrison adopted from the British reformers in the early 1830's was simply the product of the movement's closing phase; slavery in the West Indies, when finally abolished, had been softened by the cumulative effort of a half-cen-tury, an effort consistently directed from the same sources. It had begun with the outlawing of the trade (not accomplished until 1806), followed by tireless work to achieve international enforcement . . . ; from here the reformers had proceeded, in the 1820's, to a program for the meliora-tion of the plantation system itself and for the emancipation of newborn children, a part of which (but by no means all) was achieved after interminable debate in the House of Commons. In the 1830's they undertook to press for full emancipation

by means of monetary compensation and an intermedite five-year plan of appren-ticeship, a program which was passed in Commons after an item-by-item struggle in the summer of 1833. After two years the government, annoyed by the obstruc-tions of the colonial assemblies in carry-ing out the program, could finally at a stroke end slavery once and for all.

Confronted throughout by formidable opposition from Tory, military, West Indian, and High Church elements, Wil-berforce and Buxton had quite naturally moved against it with other sources of power, similarly organized. Against pro-slavery peers they could rally their own antislavery peers; against West Indian power they could oppose the interests of the East India Company; they could combat High Church instransigence, especially after Wilberforce's conversion, with the phalanx of Low Church power then at their disposal. Available to them were some of the finest legal minds of the day. Numerous reform organizations sup-ported the cause, most redoubtable of which was the London Anti-Slavery So-ciety with its royal and noble patrons, and the movement's intellectual rein-forcements (Buxton and Wilberforce were themselves men of learning and acumen) featured such names as those of Thomas Clarkson, Jeremy Stephen, and later his sons Sir James and Sir George, and the Macaulays, Zachary and his son Thomas, later Lord Macaulay. Thus bulwarked, the leaders had ample protection from pressures of sentiment on either side of them. Much of that sentiment, needless to say, was more moderate than their own, and some of it, indeed, was much more radical.

In contrast to these planners, these in-tellectuals, these men of affairs, who was poor Garrison? What matter was it that he had received the benign blessing of the dying Wilberforce? What plans had he, what were his resources—other than the impotent fury of his own poisoned pen? Where were the men of power who might have supported him a generation before (even assuming a vocabulary they could have shared, which was dubious): the Washingtons, Jeffersons, Randolphs, Henrys, Madisons, and Monroes, whose hatred of slavery had been a product not of moral abstractions but of intimate acquaintance? All were gone by the 1840's; yet it hardly mattered, for the roles which their successors might have played—the model slaveholder, the man whose wisdom had been shaped by affairs—were roles which society no longer recognized.

Our antislavery movement was for practical purposes devoid of intellectual nourishment. There was no real way for intellectual productions to avoid being democratized, no way of testing their merit other than by casting them upon the market place; the market place was where they had to pay their way. There were no limited areas within which ideas could be judged as ideas, policy as policy, and not as something else, no structure within which ideas and policies might have had their identity protected from mass pressures long enough to compete with one another rather than with moral formulas. In its ultimate stages antislavery, to reach a point where it could measurably influence public policy, had to find a lowest common denominator: the formula of "free soil." It had to be in such a form that by 1860 substantial majorities in the Northern states might be found thinking alike—sufficiently alike, at least, to bring a new party into power. By that time what little intellectual leadership antislavery had ever possessed had

long since lost control. This was the extent to which the wisdom of an Emerson was needed by the America of that generation, for all the difference it made. In such circumstances an intellectual elite—a real elite, with a clear sense of its own function and equipped to play the needed roles—could hardly have been either recruited or maintained.

The reasons for such an elite's never appearing were anything but accidental. There was no way for intellectuals to be located institutionally and thus be sensitized to power and the meaning of power. They could not conceive of competing institutions in a state of tension; tensions in that sense were not really there. No bargaining relationship could thus exist between them and the institution of slavery. Intellect itself had been "sectionalized"; the closest thing to a community of intellectuals was to be found at Concord, but such men were not national intellectuals; they had no community with Southern counterparts. Those counterparts would have been located in Virginia and elsewhere in the upper South, where slavery had already come under pressures other than those created by moral aggression from the outside.

These men, cut off from the source of power, with virtually no vested connections, far removed from that institution with which they became increasingly concerned, thus had a few tests other than their own consciences and those of their average fellow citizens, to prevent their thought from moving to the simplest of moral abstractions. The very nature of that thought—anti-institutional, individualistic, abstract, and charged with guilt—blocked off all concrete approaches to the problems of society.

Suggestions for Additional Reading

The literature available on the history of abolitionism is large. Thus, this bibliography is highly selective and should be supplemented by the excellent bibliographical essay in Louis Filler, *The Crusade Against Slavery* (New York, 1960). Filler's study, the most recent history of the movement, is a synthesis that considers connections between abolitionism and other reform movements, and attempts to measure the impact of abolitionism on the sectional crisis of the 1840s and 1850s. Other useful accounts that vary in their interpretation of the origins of abolitionism, the motivating impulses behind it, and its effects are: A. B. Hart, *Slavery and Abolition, 1831–1841* (New York, 1906); Jesse Macy, *The Anti-Slavery Crusade* (New Haven, 1921); Roman J. Zorn, "The New England Anti-Slavery Society; Pioneer Abolition Organization," in *The Journal of Negro History*, XLII (1957), 157–176; and Russell B. Nye, *William Lloyd Garrison and the Humanitarian Reformers* (Boston, 1955).

Biographies of prominent abolition figures such as Henry B. Stanton, Joshua Leavitt, William Goodell, and Elizur Wright remain to be written. However, the number of available biographies on major abolitionists is growing. The most perceptive is John L. Thomas' study of Garrison, *The Liberator: a Biography of William Lloyd Garrison* (Boston, 1963). It can be supplemented in places by W. M. Merrill, *Against Wind and Tide: a Biography of William Lloyd Garrison* (Cambridge, Mass., 1963). Other important biographical studies include: Benjamin P. Thomas, *Theodore Weld, Crusader for Freedom* (New Brunswick, N.J., 1950); Ralph V. Harlow, *Gerrit Smith, Philanthropist and Reformer* (New York, 1939); Betty Fladeland,

James Gillespie Birney: Slaveholder to Abolitionist (Ithaca, N.Y., 1955); Irving H. Bartlett, *Wendell Phillips, Brahmin Radical* (Boston, 1961); John Gill, *Tide Without Turning: Elijah P. Lovejoy and Freedom of the Press* (Boston, 1959); and Robert M. York, *George B. Cheever, Religious and Social Reformer, 1807–1890* (Orono, Me., 1955). No student of abolitionism should miss Richard Hofstadter's essay, "Wendell Phillips, the Patrician as Agitator," in *The American Political Tradition and the Men Who Made It* (New York, 1948), 135–161.

Works that analyze the relationships between evangelical ideas and the reform movements of the 1830s are numerous. Among the most important are: Timothy L. Smith, *Revivalism and Social Reform in Mid-Nineteenth Century America* (New York, 1957); Charles C. Cole, Jr., *The Social Ideas of Northern Evangelists, 1826–1860* (New York, 1954); Charles I. Foster, *An Errand of Mercy: the Evangelical United Front, 1790–1837* (Chapel Hill, N.C., 1960); John R. Bodo, *The Protestant Clergy and Public Issues, 1812–1848* (Princeton, N.J., 1954); Arthur E. Bestor, Jr., *Backwoods Utopias* (Philadelphia, 1950); Whitney R. Cross, *The Burned-Over District . . .* (Ithaca, N.Y., 1950); William G. McLoughlin, *Modern Revivalism: Charles Grandison Finney to Billy Graham* (New York, 1959); Charles R. Keller, *The Second Great Awakening in Connecticut* (New Haven, 1942); David R. Ludlum, *Social Ferment in Vermont, 1791–1850* (New York, 1939); and Clifford S. Griffin, *Their Brothers' Keeper: Moral Stewardship in the United States, 1800–1865* (New Brunswick, N.J., 1960). Other important studies that shed light on attitudes of various denominations toward slavery and abolition include Thomas E. Drake, *Quakers and Slavery in America* (New Haven, 1950); Bruce C. Staiger, "Abolitionism and the Presbyterian Schism of 1837–1838," *The Mississippi Valley Historical Review*, XXVI (1949), 391–414; and Robert Fortenbaugh, "American Lutheran Synods and Slavery, 1830–1860," *Journal of Religion*, XIII (1933), 72–92.

The relationship between British and American abolitionism needs further study. The subject can be approached, however, in Annie H. Abel and Frank J. Klingberg (eds.), *A Side-Light on Anglo-American Relations, 1839–1858* (Lancaster, Pa., 1927); and Thomas P. Martin, "The Upper Mississippi Valley in Anglo-American Anti-Slavery and Free Trade Relations, 1837–1842," *The Mississippi Valley Historical Review*, XV (1928), 204–220. Histories of the abolitionist movement in England should also be consulted. These include Reginald Coupland, *The British Anti-Slavery Movement* (London, 1933); Frank J. Klingberg, *The Anti-Slavery Movement in England* (New Haven, 1926); and William L. Mathieson, *British Slavery and Its Abolition*, 1823–1838 (London, 1926). Finally, no one should overlook Michael Kraus's perceptive essay, "Slavery Reform in the 18th Century: an Aspect of Trans-Atlantic Intellectual Cooperation," *Pennsylvania Magazine of History and Biography*, LX (1936), 53–66.

The role of the Negro in the abolitionist movement is another subject that requires further investigation. General treatments are found in John Hope Franklin, *From Slavery to Freedom: a History of American Negroes* (New York, 1947); and Leon Litwack, *The Negro in the Free States, 1790–1860* (Chicago, 1961). Litwack also examines the racial attitudes of white abolitionists. Herbert Aptheker's book, *The Negro in the Abolitionist Movement* (New York, 1943), is more comprehensive but is overdrawn and suffers from a lack of objectivity. Other studies that merit attention are: Charles H. Wesley, "The Participation of Negroes in Anti-Slavery Political Parties," *The Journal of Negro History*, XXIX (1944), 32–74; Benjamin Quarles, *Frederick Douglass* (Washington, D.C., 1948); and Philip S. Foner (ed.), *Life and Writings of Frederick Douglass* (4 vols.; New York, 1950–1955).

A number of studies, difficult to categorize, deserve attention. Among these are: Robert S. Fletcher, *A History of Oberlin College...* (2 vols.; Oberlin, Ohio, 1943); Douglas Maynard, "The World's Anti-Slavery Convention of 1840," *The Mississippi Valley Historical Review*, XL (1955), 63–76; Merton L. Dillon, "The Failure of American Abolitionists," *The Journal of Southern History*, XXV (1959), 159–177; and Benjamin Quarles, "Sources of Abolitionist Income," *The Mississippi Valley Historical Review*, XXXII (1945), 63–87.

Two articles that assess the impact of abolitionism on American labor are: Joseph G. Rayback, "The American Workingman and the Antislavery Crusade," *The Journal of Economic History*, III (1943), 152–163; and Williston H. Lofton, "Abolition and Labor," *The Journal of Negro History*, XXXIII (1948), 249–283.

Contemporary accounts, which reveal the way in which the abolitionists viewed themselves, make fascinating reading. Those with a Garrisonian bias include Oliver Johnson, *William Lloyd Garrison and His Times* (Boston, 1879); Samuel J. May, *Some Recollections of Our Anti-Slavery Conflict* (Boston, 1869); and Parker Pillsbury, *Acts of the Anti-Slavery Apostles* (Concord, N.H., 1883). See also the biography of Garrison by his sons: Francis J. Garrison and Wendell P. Garrison, *William Lloyd Garrison, 1805–1879...* (4 vols.; New York, 1885–1889). James Gillespie Birney's son wrote the major contemporary work attacking Garrison's pre-eminence. See William Birney, *James G. Birney and His Times* (New York, 1890). Other contemporary accounts by non-Garrisonian abolitionists include Henry B. Stanton, *Random Recollections* (Johnstown, N.Y., 1885); Catherine Birney, *The Grimké Sisters* (Boston, 1885); and Lewis Tappan, *The Life of Arthur Tappan* (New York,

1870). In addition, published primary source materials can be consulted with profit. For example, see Dwight L. Dumond (ed.), *The Letters of James G. Birney, 1831–1857* (2 vols.; New York, 1938); Wendell Phillips, *Speeches, Lectures, and Letters* (Boston, 1870); Henry D. Thoreau, *Anti-Slavery and Reform Papers* (London, 1890); Edward L. Pierce, *Memoir and Letters of Charles Sumner* (4 vols.; Boston and London, 1877–1893); and James Russell Lowell, *The Anti-Slavery Papers of James Russell Lowell* (2 vols.; Boston, 1902).

A comprehensive study of the rise of political abolitionism during the 1840s has not yet been written. Nor has the influence of abolitionism on the formation of the Free Soil and Republican parties received definitive treatment. Many Northern politicians who opposed the expansion of slavery for political and economic reasons did not object to the continuation of slavery in Southern states. However, some historians argue that the influence of abolitionists, direct and indirect, in molding Northern antislavery opinion was paramount. Among the more suggestive studies that bear on political abolitionism and the political antislavery movement are: Patrick W. Riddleberger, "The Making of a Political Abolitionist: George W. Julian and the Free Soilers, 1848," *Indiana Magazine of History*, LI (1955), 222–236; Joseph G. Rayback, "The Liberty Party Leaders of Ohio: Exponents of Antislavery Coalition," *Ohio Archaeological and Historical Quarterly*, LVII (1948), 165–178; Robert P. Ludlum, "Joshua Giddings, Radical," *The Mississippi Valley Historical Review*, XXIII (1936), 49–60; Reinhard H. Luthin, "Salmon P. Chase; Political Career Before the Civil War," *The Mississippi Valley Historical Review*, XXIX (1943), 517–540; George W. Julian, *The Life of Joshua R. Giddings* (Chicago, 1892); David Donald, *Lincoln's Herndon* (New York, 1948); David Donald, *Charles Sumner and the Coming of the Civil War* (New York, 1960); Charles B. Going, *David Wilmot, Free Soiler* ... (New York, 1924); Andrew W. Crandall, *The Early History of the Republican Party, 1854–1856* (Boston, 1930); Jeter A. Iseley, *Horace Greeley and the Republican Party, 1853–1861* (Princeton, N.J., 1947); Samuel Flagg Bemis, *John Quincy Adams and the Union* (New York, 1956); Frank O. Gatell, *John Gorham Palfrey and the New England Conscience* (Cambridge, Mass., 1963); Fred H. Harrington, *Fighting Politican: Major General N. P. Banks* (Philadelphia, 1948); Robert F. Durden, *James Shepherd Pike: Republicanism and the American Negro, 1850–1882* (Durham, N.C., 1957); and Richard N. Current, *Old Thad Stevens: a Study of Ambition* (Madison, Wis., 1942).

The role of abolitionism as a cause of the Civil War is an extremely controversial question that commands attention from nearly all historians of the Civil War era. A comparative analysis reflecting the views of the various schools of thought can be made by consulting a few select volumes. In addition to works from which selections appear in this book, see especially Avery O. Craven, *The Repressible Conflict, 1830–1861* (Baton Rouge, La., 1939); Arthur Y. Lloyd, *The Slavery Controversy, 1831–1860* (Chapel Hill, N.C., 1939); Dwight L. Dumond, *The Antislavery Origins of the Civil War* (Ann Arbor, Mich., 1939); Russell B. Nye, *Fettered Freedom: Civil Liberties and the Slavery Controversy, 1830–1860* (East Lansing, Mich., 1949); Kenneth M. Stampp, *And the War Came: the North and the Secession Crisis of 1860–1861* (Baton Rouge, La., 1950); Thomas J. Pressly, *Americans Interpret Their Civil War* (Princeton, N.J., 1954); Allan Nevins, *Ordeal of the Union* (2 vols.; New York, 1947); John L. Thomas, *The Liberator: a Biography of William Lloyd Garrison* (Boston, 1963); and James M. McPherson, *The Struggle for Equality: Abolitionists and the Negro in the Civil War and Reconstruction* (Princeton, N.J., 1964).